TALES FROM THE
GWLADYS
STREET

TALES FROM THE GWLADYS STREET

Stories from players and fans chronicling more than 50 years of Everton FC

JONATHAN MUMFORD & DAVID CREGEEN
Foreword by **GRAEME SHARP**

SPORTS
BOOKS

Published in Great Britain by
SportsBooks Limited
PO Box 422
Cheltenham
GL50 2YN
United Kingdom

Tel: 01242 256755
email: info@sportsbooks.ltd.uk
www.sportsbooks.ltd.uk

First published October 2009
Second edition December 2010

Cover design by Alan Hunns

A catalogue record for this book is available from
the British Library.

ISBN 978 1899807 89 5

Printed by Thomson Litho Ltd, East Kilbride, Scotland

Contents

About the authors

David Cregeen first visited Goodison Park in 1981. The humour and passion shown by the fans that day convinced him to support the Blues and he has followed Everton ever since.

After a spell in the Royal Navy, David became a college lecturer and now works as a PE teacher. He is a qualified football coach and helps coach the Merseyside Schools' FA under-18 team.

David, who has written articles for academic journals and fitness magazines, lives in Liverpool with his wife Cheryl and their eight-year-old boys, Jonathon and Thomas, who have, along with their Dad, season tickets for the family enclosure.

Jonathan Mumford's first experience of watching Everton was the 1989 FA Cup final. That day, in his adolescent naivety, he was at Wembley as a Liverpool fan. With strong guidance from his father, Steve, he saw sense and became an Evertonian.

A keen sportsman, Jonathan represented England at badminton as a junior and has recently completed his first marathon but following Everton is his first passion.

A languages teacher, he lives in Liverpool with his wife, Victoria, and is a season ticket holder in the legendary Gwladys Street end at Goodison Park.

Foreword

When growing up in Scotland, I knew Everton was a big club with quality players, but little about its fans.

However, after signing for Everton in 1980, I quickly learned how passionate they were and how much the club meant to them. When I first arrived, I lived in digs with a family of Evertonians who described the level of expectancy associated with the famous number 9 jersey, as did many supporters I met on the street. This was further reinforced when training with Colin Harvey. As a local lad who had played for the Blues, Colin was quick to stamp his authority on the young players, emphasising the importance of wearing the royal blue jersey. Colin stressed to us how Everton fans demanded nothing less than 100 per cent and that was what you had to give, whether it was a Central League game against Bury or a First Division tie against Manchester United. If fans saw you were giving your all, then they would take to you.

On pre-season trips to Europe in the '80s I began to see for myself just how incredible the supporters were. We would travel to far-flung places in the middle of nowhere to play against Third Division teams, yet fans would be there in numbers. We once travelled to Dordrecht in Holland, a place nobody had heard of, yet, as always, fans were there before us. It was fantastic to see them and listen to their incredible stories of how they had got there. You knew then that you were representing something special.

We shared a mutual respect for each other and, on many occasions, the players used them as a '12th man' to help us in important games. Stoke City's Victoria Ground was an intimidating place to play but it was made less hostile by the thousands that followed us for the FA Cup game in 1984. Their passion inspired us to victory that day and propelled the team into the most successful period in the club's history.

The importance of our fans was perhaps best illustrated when Bayern Munich came to Goodison for the second leg of the European Cup Winners' Cup semi-final. We followed our usual pre-match routine, which was to travel to the ground a couple of hours before kick-off. As we approached Goodison Park, I sensed something different. Normally the streets before kick-off were quiet, but for this game, they were jam-packed. As the team bus turned onto Gwladys Street, we were greeted by a mass of blue which brought the coach to a standstill. There was a great atmosphere which continued as fans entered the ground. That night the place was bouncing.

During the game, even when we went a goal down, with the fans behind us, we felt we weren't out of it.

At half-time, Howard Kendall just said 'Get it into the box and the Gwladys Street will suck it into the net,' and it felt like they did.

My in-laws, who were Celtic fans, also attended this landmark game. They had witnessed all of Celtic's big European nights but afterwards said that they had never experienced anything like it before.

Throughout my long association with Everton, I have come to realise how important the club is to the fans and how important the fans are to the club. Evertonians are knowledgeable about their proud history, something which is ingrained. Their incredible loyalty, both at home and abroad, even during difficult times, means they are up there with the best of them. Everton weddings and funerals show how, for many, Everton Football Club is not just a part of their life – it is their life.

A special club with special fans, Everton really is the team to follow.

Graeme Sharp
Everton FC Fans' Relations Manager

The 1950s

On the last day of the 1950–51 season, Everton were struggling at the bottom of the First Division in a lowly 20th position, just two points ahead of Chelsea and Sheffield Wednesday. With their destiny in their own hands, Everton travelled to Hillsborough requiring just a point to stay up. However, Everton lost the match 6-0 while Chelsea won their final game 4-0; results that placed all three teams on 32 points. In those days, relegation was decided by goal average, as opposed to goal difference, and Everton were relegated by just 0.04 of a goal.

As a Second Division team, the following season's attempts to regain their top-flight status ended miserably. They managed to finish 16th, the lowest in the club's proud history. On a positive note, however, they reached the semi-final of the FA Cup and were narrowly beaten 4-3 by Bolton Wanderers, who had led 4-0 at half-time. In addition, Everton had signed charismatic centre-forward Dave Hickson from Ellesmere Port, who would later become known affectionately as 'The Cannonball Kid'.

Two years later, in their final game of the 1953–54 season, Everton needed to beat Oldham Athletic at Boundary Park to secure promotion back to the First Division. Lying second behind Leicester City, Everton needed to beat Oldham 6-0 to ensure that they not only returned to the top flight, but as champions on goal average.

Percy Rigby was one of many fans who saw the game that night.

Oldham v Everton, 29 April 1954
Back Where We Belong by Percy Rigby

I travelled up to Boundary Park in April 1954, with my cousin, George Burnett, who was playing in goal for Oldham in this re-arranged evening fixture. It was a warm summer's day and thousands of Everton supporters had made the trip up the East Lancs. Road, many of whom were without tickets. Local radio had declared the game a sell-out and advised fans without tickets against travelling. However, many chose to ignore the warnings in the hope of seeing Everton not just return to the First Division, but hopefully as champions.

Before joining Oldham, my cousin George had spent 13 years with Everton during the forties and fifties, playing alongside the likes of Joe Mercer and Harry Catterick. He had, in fact, left Everton several years prior to joining Oldham to sign for Ellesmere Port, but had his contract ripped up so he could return to Goodison Park to deputise for Everton's first-choice keeper Ted Sagar and his reserve, who were both injured.

When we arrived at Oldham's ground I took my match ticket from George, went for a few pints with my mates and then made my way into the ground, standing behind the goal where the Everton supporters were massed. There were high walls around Boundary Park to keep out fans without tickets, but in certain areas the walls were lower. Everton fans without tickets took advantage of these vulnerable spots and used any means they could, including cars, to scramble over the wall and into the ground. Once they made it to the top of the wall, fans inside created a space below on to which they could drop. To combat this problem, police on horseback spread tar from large drums on to the walls to deter others from entering. Not to be outdone by this deterrent, quick-thinking Evertonians placed Liverpool Echos over the tar to protect themselves as they leapt over and on to the terraces.

Prior to the game, knowing George Burnett was a former Everton player and that Everton needed to win 6-0 to win the division, people were saying to me 'He'll let six in for you.'

At half-time, with Everton leading 4-0, I was beginning to think they might be right, although knowing George, I know he wouldn't have tried to do Everton any favours. Everton themselves failed to build on this advantage when they missed a penalty in the second half to make it 5-0. With that, they lost the chance to become champions, although they won the game 4-0 and were promoted as runners-up on 56 points, one point ahead of Blackburn Rovers.

At the final whistle, jubilant Evertonians streamed out of the ground and into the nearby pubs to celebrate. Several hours later, we put down our glasses and began our journey home. Not many people had cars in those days but those who did beeped their horns and fans hung out of car windows as we celebrated being back where we belonged. To make the occasion extra special, that same season Liverpool were relegated from the First Division and remained in the Second Division for eight years. Happy days!

Although Everton were once again in the First Division, they struggled under the leadership of former Everton and England half-back Cliff Britton. Britton, who won the FA Cup as a player with Everton in 1933, resigned as manager in 1956 under pressure from the board.

After two and a half years under Ian Buchan, on 1 October 1958, former Manchester United player Johnny Carey was appointed manager, the year Everton suffered the biggest defeat in their history, a 10-4 loss to Spurs at White Hart Lane on 11 October, in Bill Nicholson's first match in charge of the London club.

I was running back to the centre circle after I scored the second goal against Liverpool and pure elation welled up inside me. I remember thinking, I just love this place – I want this place for ever.

Alan Ball, August 1966

The 1960s

Although Everton's best league position under Carey was 11th, in 1960, the Irishman was responsible for bringing to Goodison three players who would play important roles in reviving the club's fortunes – Alex Young, Roy Vernon and Jimmy Gabriel.

Alex Young was signed from Hearts for a fee in the region of £40,000. An instinctive footballer, Young produced moments of such skill and flair that he became a cult hero among fans, who named him 'The Golden Vision'.

Vernon, a future Everton captain, was signed from Blackburn Rovers for a fee of £27,000 while 19-year-old Gabriel, a strong and energetic right-half, joined from Dundee.

In 1960–61, these three helped Everton finish fifth, their best league position since their League Championship success in 1938–39. But despite the progress made under Carey, chairman John Moores wasn't satisfied and sacked him in the back of a taxi the pair had taken after a Football League AGM in London. Over the next few years, when Everton's performances failed to meet expectations, fans would shout 'Send for a taxi' in reference to Carey's peculiar exit.

John Moores wanted Everton to return to the top by playing attractive football and installed Harry Catterick in an attempt to bring silverware back to Goodison. Catterick, a former Everton player, guided Everton to fourth place in his first season and the following year led them to their sixth League Championship. During a season of bad weather,

Roy Vernon and Alex Young scored more than 20 goals each, a feat not achieved since. For their stylish brand of football, Everton became known as 'The School of Science'. They didn't drop lower than third, were undefeated at home and lost only six of their 42 league matches, winning the league by six points.

Everton finished third and fourth in the next two seasons but in 1965–66, Catterick tinkered with the team and Everton dropped to a disappointing 11th. Following Everton in the league and cup that year was a young school-boy who, in later years, would play for his beloved Blues.

Blackpool v Everton, 15 January 1966
Ball on the Beach by Mike Lyons

I started going to Goodison Park with my dad and my brother when I was about eight. We had season tickets for The Paddock and would watch the games stood just in front of the letters that displayed the half-time scores from the other games going on.

Towards the end of the 1965–66 season I was only 14 but had started going to some games with just my mates. On Saturday, 15 January, around four of us decided to watch Everton play at Blackpool and, after playing football for our school, De La Salle in the morning we caught the Ribble bus from Skelhorne Street to Blackpool.

When we arrived the bus dropped us off miles from the ground. It was still early in the morning, too early to go to the match so as we had a bit of time to kill we made our way down to the beach to make the most of our day out. As we were walking along the beach we noticed someone with red hair who seemed to be out for a leisurely stroll. When I spotted him I shouted 'Hey look, there's Alan Ball.' Sure enough it was Bally, so we went over to him for a chat and his autograph. Bally told us that he was just out for a walk on the beach to clear his head before the game, something he would often perform as part of his pre-match routine.

Weeks earlier, I'd seen him play for England under-23s against Bulgaria at Goodison Park and knew what a good player he was, so we began trying to persuade him to join us. 'You're a great player, you. Why don't you come to Everton?' we said, insisting he joined the Blues. We probably got on his nerves a bit but he was very polite and took the time to chat to us.

Eventually, after walking along the beach and paying him many compliments we left Bally to continue his pre-match preparations before making our way to Bloomfield Road. Probably the most notable memory of the game was the fact that it was Joe Royle's debut. Not only was this significant because Joe was just 16, and at the time Everton's youngest ever debutant, he was also making his debut at the expense of fans' favourite, Alex Young – 'The Golden Vision'. Many fans were incensed at Young's omission as his stunning skills had helped Everton to the 1962–63 Championship, making him a crowd idol. As a consequence of dropping Young, coupled with Everton's 2-0 defeat on the day, Everton manager Harry Catterick allegedly became the victim of an assault by disgruntled Everton supporters.

Happily though, later that year everything worked out well for all parties when England and Alan Ball won the World Cup and we reached the FA Cup final. I never asked Alan Ball whether he remembered us that day or whether we influenced his decision to join Everton but I'm not half glad he did. I had the pleasure to be a teammate of his during his time at Everton and a lasting memory I have of him is a pair of his trademark white Hummel boots he generously gave me.

Despite their poor league form that season, in 1966 Everton reached their first FA Cup final in 33 years.

On the road to Wembley, Everton defeated both Manchester teams. It took three attempts to defeat City while United were beaten 1-0 in the semi-final, the winner scored by Colin Harvey. Before Everton played United, they faced Leeds United in a league match at Elland Road and fielded an entire reserve team, for which they were fined £2,000 by the Football League. On reaching the final, Everton became the first side in 63 years to do so without conceding a goal while their opponents, Sheffield Wednesday, reached Wembley without playing at home.

Before the final, manager Harry Catterick surprised Everton fans by selecting the virtually unknown Mike Trebilcock in his starting line-up. Trebilcock, a £20,000 mid-season buy from Plymouth Argyle, was chosen ahead of Fred Pickering, who had also been left out for the semi-final with Trebilcock again being preferred, despite scoring in every round previously. Pickering, a former England international and Everton's top scorer that season, must have been disappointed to be left out in favour of Trebilcock, whose name wasn't even in the Wembley programme. However, the rest, as they say, is history.

Here, fans and former players remember one of the best finals in FA Cup history.

With Manchester City it was a love affair, but with Everton it's more like a marriage.

Howard Kendall

FA Cup Final, Everton v Sheffield Wednesday, 14 May 1966
A Belter of a Cup Final by Dave Walsh

I was 13 and had managed to hang on to my wages from working Saturday mornings on Paddy's Market, Cazneau Street. I had a ten-bob note but no ticket for the final. I crept out of the house after dinner on Friday night, without telling my mum (which incurred an immediate death sentence in those days) and had a quick look at the school atlas. After taking several buses, it was midnight. I was at Spittle Crossroads, on the A41, Whitchurch to be exact, looking to head southwards, more specifically to London, Wembley, to see the Boys in Blue.

There wasn't a lot of traffic at that time of night, but, decked out in my scarf and home-made rosette, I soon got myself into central London, arriving at about 5 a.m. Not having the foggiest idea where Wembley was I had to ask directions and then I started to walk.

I arrived at about 6.30 a.m. and it was as dead as a dodo. There was absolutely no one about except men with a lorry delivering big, shiny, new bins. I saw them go inside and my plan to get into the match began to take shape. I waited until they had carried out their delivery and then, when all seemed cushty, I pulled along the sliding gates as far as I could and got into Wembley through one of those elongated diamond shapes that was a bit broken. It was a bit tight to say the least, but it worked. I hid in one of these bins for about five hours, barely daring to breathe as more and more workers came in. Just when I thought the coast was clear, and I could climb out and mingle with the crowds, I was rumbled by a police patrol with dogs that started barking as soon as they came near my cunning hiding place. I was dragged out by the lughole and promptly thrown out.

I tried a few more times over the next few hours to get back in through the same hole, but quickly realised there was no chance. Scuffers everywhere. In desperation, just before the game started, I jumped the turnstile, having had tons of practice bunking into the Goodison Park Boys' Pen for years. I was in. In no time I'd dodged my way into the Everton end and watched the game. We won, of course, with the greatest comeback I will probably ever see.

After spending some time singing and shouting down Wembley Way, I finally started the trek home. The return journey was by motorway, much more difficult and a lot longer than I'd anticipated. I'm not sure if there were any Little Chefs or Trust House Fortes in those days but I never saw one.

Finally, late Sunday night, I arrived home to face the music. The back door was usually open in those days, locked with only a latch. I went in to take my well-deserved beating with the belt, probably the buckle end for serious crimes such as this. They were all waiting;

Mum, Dad, six assorted brothers and sisters, a couple of odd aunts and uncles and a handful of nosey neighbours.

I avoided the usual good hiding. This was only because my mum was waving a copy of The News of the World or The People, I can't remember which, and there I was on the front page, clear as day, getting thrown out by several large bizzies!

So I had to ditch the planned feeble excuse I'd thought might save me and hold my hands up. (I'd hidden my scarf and rosette, programme etc. under a stone in the back jigger). I had to admit that I had gone to Wembley to watch Everton win the Cup.

The good hiding came the next day (buckle end!).

"Every time I score, the passion comes out and I try to relay that back to the fans and to the players and the staff at how grateful I am to be playing for such a good football club. I am part of the furniture at Everton but I don't take it for granted. No money in this world could convince me to play for Liverpool. It's respect for the Everton supporters. You just can't do that. It goes against everything I stand for. Once you've played for Everton and know what it means to be a Blue then you know what it means to beat Liverpool."

Tim Cahill, *Sport and Style*, April 2009

Honeymoon Blues by Paul Dougherty

I got married on 7th May 1966! Everton were due to play Sheffield Wednesday on the 14th. Unbeknown to my new bride, I had been exploring how to get a ticket but with no success.

Then out of the blue (!) came the possibility that my cousin, who lived in Harrow, near London, might be able to get one but he would not know until Friday, 13 May.

My wife and I were going to the Norfolk Broads for a week's honeymoon, so I was in a bit of a quandary. However, during the honeymoon, after a few drinks for Dutch courage I approached the subject and fortunately my wife insisted that if the ticket was available, then I should go.

I rang my cousin and he had managed to get me a ticket from a guy who worked for him who was going out with the daughter of a director of Brighton and Hove Albion. This now meant leaving my wife of seven days, driving from Norwich to Harrow to get the ticket and going to the match.

I then rang my four mates back in Liverpool to tell them I would be going. Graham Harcombe, Derek Baswava, Dave Crowley and Dave Gibson were lads I used to meet up with in the Old Roan pub, Aintree, for a few pints before the game. The lads were intending to drive down during the night so we arranged a meeting place. They were planning to have a few drinks at The Vermont Club, in London Street, just off London Road (now gone) before setting off. Four guys, two tickets!

All went well and I met them in a pub near London's Victoria Station. Imagine my surprise when I saw they'd brought Dave Crowley's brother, Jeff, a fanatical Reds supporter! They'd got him pissed on the Friday night in the Vermont Club, stuck him in their car and he had woken up in London. We now had three tickets, six blokes. As resourceful Scousers, we weren't going to let a little thing like that stop us from watching the Blues, and we formulated a plan. At the ticket gate I went first, showed my ticket and a pound note to the man at the turnstile and gave him a wink. He took the note, and gave me back the ticket which I passed to my mate behind me. This was repeated three times and we were all in. Remember, back then it was standing on the terraces so fans without tickets could often bunk in one way or another.

Mission accomplished, we saw a great Everton side turn a 2-0 deficit into a 3-2 victory and we were there thanks, dare I say, to my wife, to whom I am still married – and I still have the programme.

Goodison Goes to Wembley by Percy Rigby

I went to Wembley in '66 with several mates, one of whom was Billy Halliwell, a coppersmith who worked at Harland and Wolff on the Dock Road.

On the Friday night before the final, we met up with Billy at Harland and Wolff's social club on Hawthorne Road, Bootle, where Billy also worked as a steward. Billy had agreed to drive his car down to London and when we arrived at the club he called us over to it.

'Here ye are,' he said as he unveiled the car in which we would be travelling to Wembley.

To our surprise, Billy had hand-crafted a model of Goodison Park which he had then mounted on to the top of the car. It was a cracking model that even had floodlights and grass in the middle of it on which were little blue Subbuteo men.

After admiring his handiwork for several minutes, Billy then revealed the model's 'pièce de résistance'.

'Look at this,' he said, at which point he flicked a switch on the car dashboard which in turn switched on the floodlights of the Goodison Park model.

Laughing at our mascot, we piled into Billy's car and set off for London along with our very own floodlit Goodison Park.

When we arrived on the Friday night, we parked the car by Harrow-on-the-Hill where we had booked a hotel. We left the car and the model in Harrow, from where you could see Wembley Stadium, not expecting to see the model again, or at least in the same condition.

When we woke up on Cup final day, to our surprise the model was still there and in perfect condition – a good omen we thought.

In good spirits, we took the tube into London to watch the final. However, we were solemn at 2-0 down. The place erupted when we pulled it back to 2-1, then 2-2 and when Derek Temple came running towards us behind that goal and made it 3-2, euphoria set in. After an unbelievable game, we ended up celebrating at the

Chelsea Supporters' Club where we had a cracking time before staying the night in the capital.

The following day we made our way back to Harrow, again, not expecting to see the model in one piece. However, there it was, 'Goodison Park' in all its glory, unscathed and floodlights still working.

Still happy after seeing one of Everton's finest performances, we made our way back to Liverpool. On our way home we decided to continue our celebrations by stopping off for a few pints in Wolverhampton. When we stopped I thought 'This is where our luck will run out. If it's gonna go, it'll definitely go here.' But, after quenching our thirst, we returned to the car to find 'Goodison Park' still in A1 condition.

From Wolverhampton, we drove back to Liverpool with the Goodison Park model which was left along with the car at the social club while we took the bus to County Road to watch Everton's victory parade.

I don't know what happened to our very own Goodison Park but the Old Lady certainly brought us luck that memorable day in May.

In later years, Percy shared his extensive football knowledge and memories with listeners of BBC Radio Merseyside when he assisted Alan Jackson between 1998 and 2005 on the much-loved Football Football Show.

Don't Call Me Cassius by Phil Henders

I started watching football in the 1940s along with my six brothers, two of whom were Reds, the others being Evertonians. To begin with, like lots of fans of that generation, I actually followed both teams as it was something to do on a Saturday afternoon, although as time went on I became an out-and-out Evertonian.

In 1965–66 I followed Everton in every round of the FA Cup. In the third round we were drawn against non-league Bedford Town. It was a big occasion for them but we managed to win 3-0.

After the match we went for a few pints and ended up gatecrashing Bedford Town Hall where we had a drink with the Bedford Town players. We were chatting with their captain, a centre half named Kenny, about the game and he slated Everton's centre forward Fred Pickering, calling him a 'camel' despite the fact he had scored one of Everton's goals that day.

By the time we left for home we were 'well-oiled' and on the journey back it started to snow. Conditions became worse and we could hardly see where we were headed. We hadn't realised we had driven past Liverpool and were headed towards Newcastle when thick snow and an empty petrol tank brought us to a halt. I started arguing with my brother Tony about whose fault it was and the pair of us ended up boxing at the side of the road in the snow.

Our sparring was brought to an abrupt halt when a copper arrived. We explained that we'd run out of petrol and to our relief he said he'd help us. He contacted a local garage and a bloke arrived soon after with enough petrol to make it back to Liverpool. The copper even gave us a short escort to help us on our way and we eventually arrived home.

My three Evertonian brothers, Raymond, Adrian and Tony, and I made sure we were all at the final even though none of us had a ticket! When we pulled in at Euston station we headed for Covent Garden for some breakfast and a few pints which was standard routine when visiting the capital for a game, before beginning our search for tickets. We managed to get one at face-value from a genuine Everton supporter and purchased a more expensive one for the stands but we were still two short.

At Wembley we each slipped the fella on the turnstile a ten-bob note and he let us in. However, there was a further barrier inside the ground where you had to show your ticket again to a steward before they would let you go further. To overcome this second hurdle, fans without tickets had to wait inside one of the toilets until one of their mates with a match ticket could come and collect them. The supporter on the terraces would take his ticket and borrow one from an Evertonian before going to the toilets. There he would pass one of the tickets to the fan hiding in the cubicle and both would show their tickets before walking on to the terraces. We did exactly the same and it wasn't long before we were inside. The official attendance was 100,000 but, like us, thousands more managed to get in by one way or another.

Jubilant scenes greeted the final whistle after we had overturned what seemed to be the impossible. To celebrate, we decided to go for a meal and a few pints. We ended up near Trafalgar Square where Everton fans had poured blue dye into the fountains. Men dressed in their best suits jumped fully clothed into the royal blue water and other Evertonians danced in the streets. Even Sheffield Wednesday supporters joined us in our finest hour.

From Trafalgar Square, we headed to Soho where more Evertonians had gathered. A big fella shouted 'Come on, join on,' encouraging fans to form a 'conga', which they did. The chain of dancing Evertonians stretched back as far as the eye could see and the leaders made their way into a striptease club. The club doorman stood aside, powerless to stop the ever-growing line of fans. We danced down the stairs and into the club singing, much to the shock of the club's clientele, before exiting through a fire door and back on to the streets. Once the chain dispersed we moved on in search of a café. As we neared the Piccadilly Hotel an Evertonian shouted to us 'Hey lads, Cassius Clay is in there and he's signing autographs.'

Without hesitation, we shot into the hotel where, sure enough, the heavyweight champion of the world, in London to fight Britain's Henry Cooper, was standing in the foyer with his sparring partner, Jimmy Ellis, who later held the world title when Ali was banned. Smartly dressed, looking relaxed and fit, the champion signed autographs for all the Evertonians, turning nobody away. When it was our turn, my brother Raymond went first. Raymond had been a good footballer, who had represented Great Britain Youth and Everton Colts, but his career was ended after he contracted TB while on National Service.

As Raymond approached he handed over his match programme.

'Can I have your autograph please, Cass?'

The huge figure collected his matchday souvenir and with pen in hand began to scribe. 'Not Cassius,' he said while writing. 'That's my name'; and he pointed to Raymond's autographed programme which read Muhammad Ali. He then signed my Wembley song sheet and any other pieces of paper lads could get their hands on.

In later years I couldn't dedicate as much time to following Everton as I had begun to own and breed racehorses. As I lived in Crosby, one of my horses was called Crosby Triangle and it won four of its first five races.

At a meeting in Ayr, Crosby Triangle romped home in the first race of the afternoon. Bob Hope, the Hollywood comedian, attended the meeting but arrived late for the first race. When he saw that a horse with the name Crosby had won a race he had missed, he said, with an ironic reference to his former sidekick Bing Crosby, 'God, that man haunts me.'

Perhaps Bob Hope should have followed Everton instead of the horses, as being an Evertonian you can't lose.

We were one down at half-time, then they scored just after, so it does go through your mind that it's 'maybe next year' and it was a heck of a comeback. Mike Trebilcock did well for us that day. The funny thing about Wembley was all the Evertonians outside drinking beer, and they want to be where you are and you want to be where they are! Meeting Princess Margaret, who I like to think of as an Evertonian, it was a great day.

Brian Labone, Evertonfc.com, May 2006

Beyond My Wildest Dreams by Ray Parr

I travelled to Wembley with my dad to watch what was my first Cup final. I didn't have a ticket but my dad did, so we searched all over the place for another. Eventually my dad managed to buy one in the toilets outside Wembley for fifteen shillings, 75 pence in today's money but three times the face value of a ticket at that time.

I remember being dressed in a blue and white scarf and wearing my builder's hard hat which had a mini replica of the FA Cup on top of it.

It was an amazing occasion. Entering the stadium I was full of confidence as Everton were favourites to lift the trophy, although at two-nil down I felt terrible, really down in the dumps.

Anyway, we bounced back to win, which was absolutely incredible, and being a lifelong Evertonian I was so excited about the whole thing.

After the team lifted the FA Cup we left the ground and headed off to my uncle's in Tottenham to stay the night as we couldn't afford the cost of a hotel in London. I turned up for a drink in a local British Legion club still dressed as I was for the final and singing all our songs so the locals must have thought I was mad. I suppose it would be the same if a Spurs fan turned up in a bar in Scotty Road in the same manner if they had won the final!!

If I'd have thought that night, that many years later I would talk to one of those who played in '66, I would have been 'over the moon'. If somebody had told me I would end up with one of the winners' medals, I'd have just laughed. However, that's what happened. Around ten years ago, not only did I speak to one of the players, I also acquired his winners' medal.

Around 1998, the Liverpool Echo ran an article about Brian Harris who was man-of-the-match that day. Brian was the player who put on the policeman's helmet after it had fallen off the officer while he pursued Eddie Cavanagh, after Eddie had run on to the Wembley turf to celebrate Everton's comeback. The article reported how Brian had fallen on hard times and as a result, wanted to sell his '66 medal as well as his 1969–70 League Championship medal.

After reading the article, I immediately got in touch with Brian and told him I'd like to buy them. I asked him how much he wanted, and he said he didn't really know. I told him the best thing to do was to have them valued by someone like Bonhams or Christie's who have specialist sections to deal with such items.

I explained that, at the end of the day, at auction he could get half of their valuation if there were no Everton fans in attendance, but then again he could get twice their valuation; it would depend on who was bidding that day. If two wealthy Evertonians wanted them, they could fetch anything.

Brian said he didn't know how to do it so I offered to do it for him and pay him the top valuation. I contacted both companies, obtained written valuations and paid Brian the highest valuation received. As I promised Brian I will never reveal the amount.

Brian's medals now have pride of place in my football collection, a tangible reminder of one of Everton's greatest days.

Colin Harvey was born and raised in the Fazakerley area of Liverpool and grew up supporting Everton. As a young boy, he would attend Goodison Park on Saturday afternoons with his brother Brian and watch the Blues from the boys' pen while his dad Jim stood on the Gwladys Street. Like Colin, his dad was Everton through-and-through and present when Everton regained their top-flight status when they defeated Oldham in 1954. Delighted at their return to the First Division, Jim Harvey had even returned home with a unique memento: a piece of the match turf which he presented to Colin the following day. Colin fulfilled his childhood ambition when he signed for Everton in 1962 and a year later, aged just 18, made his Everton debut against Inter Milan in the San Siro Stadium in the preliminary round of the European Cup.

In May 1966 Colin was in the Everton FA Cup final team. Here he remembers this historic occasion.

Joe the Raconteur by Colin Harvey

We travelled to London on the Thursday night before the final and drove straight to Wembley for a look round and to walk on the pitch. None of the players had played at Wembley before although I had been there the year before when Liverpool had beaten Leeds United 2-1. I had a mate who was a Liverpudlian and I'd managed to get two tickets so went along with him. I remember thinking then that it would be a dream to play in the Cup final and just a year later there I was.

After a tour of Wembley, we travelled on to Selsdon Park, a hotel that had been used over the years by many teams playing in Wembley finals. Selsdon Park had been a family home that had been converted into a hotel. We stayed there on the Thursday night, and on the Friday morning we trained at the back of the hotel adjacent to its magnificent golf course. After we had finished our training session we spent the rest of the day relaxing at the hotel.

On the day of the final we travelled by coach. Driving down Wembley Way I could see thousands of people making their way to the stadium. There were thousands of Evertonians, many of whom I recognised. I noticed my mum and dad, a couple of uncles and my granddad. We drove past the crowds, into the stadium and went upstairs to the changing rooms.

The dressing rooms at Wembley were huge, and about an hour and a half before the game we started to get changed. Each player had their own particular superstitions or routines before the game to help them prepare. Some players would put their left boot on first; some would put their shirts on just before they were due to go out on to the field. Whatever you did you tried to keep as much to your normal routine as possible. In the changing area I was sat quite near to Tommy Wright, a good friend of mine. We had joined Everton together from school when we were kids and there were only a few weeks between our birthdays. We were the youngest players in the team at just 21 and our careers had followed similar paths.

As the players were getting into their pre-match routines I was just getting on with things, trying to focus. Other players were more vocal but I got on with things in my own quiet way. TV cameras were present but I didn't realise they were filming us until I watched the footage some time after the game. It was quite unlike Harry Catterick, the manager, to allow cameras into the dressing room as he wasn't a media-friendly person. This was possibly something that prevented him receiving the recognition and publicity he deserved. People talked of big names at the time like Don Revie, Bill Shankly and Bill Nicholson but Harry was up there with them. He had won the league with Everton in 1963 and would have more success with Everton in years to come.

The mood in the dressing room about an hour before kick-off was quite sombre. The room we were in was around 40 to 50 feet above ground level so fans down below couldn't look in on the players. It was a warm late spring day and the changing room window was open to let in fresh air. Just as I was changing, a head popped through the window and a voice shouted, 'Hey Colin, have you got any tickets?'

I recognised the face straight away. It was a lad I had grown up with in Fazakerley, Joe O'Donoghue. Joe had scaled up the drainpipe outside the dressing room window in a desperate attempt to see the game. After hearing him say that I just started to laugh and the rest of the team fell about too. Joe's appearance brought the place down.

I had known Joe since I was about three or four, and had grown up with him and another family called the Browns. Joe was a real raconteur and a great character. If you were out in his company he would always have a story to tell and a different voice for each one. Most of the families who lived in Fazakerley had moved from Scotland Road and we all loved football. I remember on one occasion I had been away with the England under-23s on an end of season tour playing against Greece, Bulgaria and Turkey. On the day I arrived back from the ten-day tournament I knew there would be a game on, so later that evening I went straight round to the field by the British Legion where I knew the lads would be playing. Sure enough there was a match going on with around 14 a side and I just joined in, as you did.

After breaking the ice with his comical interruption, I think Joe was ordered down by the police and we were left to carry on with our preparations. Before I knew it we were walking out at Wembley, the hymns and National Anthem were being played and the whistle to start the match was blown.

With 33 minutes of the game remaining and trailing Sheffield Wednesday 2-0, my granddad had had enough and decided to leave. We ourselves thought it was all over until Trebs (Mike Trebilcock) came up with two important goals. My granddad managed to get back into Wembley at 2-2 to see the winner from Derek Temple and Everton lift the cup. Joe O'Donoghue had somehow managed to wangle his way in to see the game too but don't ask me how!

The day after one of the greatest comebacks in FA Cup history, we travelled back to Liverpool and, after a tour of the city to parade the trophy, I went back to my mum's house in Manica Crescent. By the time I arrived, along with Trebs, the party was in full swing and it seemed like all of Fazakerley had turned up too. A friend of mine from Scotland Road, who worked at a brewery, had managed to get hold of some beer and people were in good voice as well as spirits. It was really busy in my mum's so I had to go next door to watch on television the team's celebrations with the cup. I'd brought my cup winner's medal to our house and got it out to show people. I was a bit drunk and it was getting passed round from person to person but I didn't have to worry. My mum, who wasn't a drinker, had clocked everyone who touched the medal and took it from the last person to hold it. My mum kept hold of the medal from that day in 1966 and it was only returned to me about 12 years ago when she sadly passed away.

Once Everton has touched you nothing will be the same.

Alan Ball

The Moorfields Donkey by Terry Darracott

In 1966, aged 15, I signed as an apprentice for Everton. As a young-ster I had represented Liverpool schoolboys and had the chance to sign for Liverpool or Everton but chose Everton, my boyhood team. It was a dream come true for me and my family and a great honour to learn from such great professionals. As an apprentice it was my job to put out the first team kit in the dressing room and clean the boots of Colin Harvey and Tommy Wright. Both these players and the rest of the first team squad were great examples to young apprentices. For ourselves, we had to train until 5 p.m. but the senior players could go home after lunch. However, they all put in extra work and joined us on the training ground in the afternoons. I remember watching their extra effort and thinking, that's what you had to do to make it in the first team. If it was good enough for them, then it was good enough for me.

As guests of the club, all the apprentices and young pros travelled to Wembley that year to watch the final. I had never been to London before so I was in awe of the place and the occasion. We stayed along with other guests of Everton in Russell Square, allowing the team to prepare at Selsdon Park.

During the final, I remember thinking how good it would be to play in a game such as this although, after half-time when we were trailing 2-0, I was deflated, thinking we were beaten.

In the second half, though, the team produced their almighty comeback. It was a game I have subsequently watched around a million times on DVD.

When I arrived back in Liverpool the following day I spoke to my parents and family about the whole experience. During our conver-sation my mum asked, 'Did you hear about what your Uncle Mickey did?'

I hadn't heard anything so said, 'No, what?'

My uncle, Mickey Keaton, was a great character and great

Evertonian from Scotland Road. He was fanatical about Everton and went to every game home and away. A gang of his pals had been to the final and when they arrived home on the Sunday, they went to the Wine Lodge in Moorfields where they used to drink. In those days there were two large entrances to the Wine Lodge and it was rumoured that the Liverpool fans drank on the left-hand side while the Evertonians drank on the right and people kept to their side depending on which team they followed. Don't ask me how, where, or why, but my Uncle Mickey had managed to get hold of a donkey and had dressed it up in all blue and white. He then took it to the Wine Lodge, which was filled to capacity, walked in through the left-hand door and paraded it through the left-hand side where all the Liverpudlians drank, before exiting on the right. Naturally this caused chaos as he was cheered on one side and slaughtered on the other; not that it would have bothered him as he was a smashing guy who was renowned for doing mad things.

Thankfully I progressed through the ranks at Everton and enjoyed many more memorable occasions during my long association with the club.

In September 1968, I made my Everton debut aged 17 against Arsenal at Goodison Park, deputising for the injured World Cup winner Ray Wilson. Ray was another great player and professional I learned so much from by just observing from a distance and when I stood in for him in the 2-0 victory I became the youngest player to play for Everton at Goodison Park.

It took me another couple of years to get more starts, one of which was an evening game against Manchester United at Goodison. At the time Man United had a great side and before the game I was asked by Harry Catterick to man-mark George Best. The Catt asked me, did I want to track him just to the halfway line and pick him up when he entered our half, or just follow him everywhere. Being 19 at the time I wasn't bothered, but opted to follow him wherever he went.

I started the game in central midfield as Bestie never had a set position and would drift all over the park. Being an out-and-out defender this role suited me and I put in some strong challenges to try to stop him playing, for which I was warned by the referee. Following Bestie took me all over the park and on one occasion I found myself in the left back position. I took possession of the ball, turned inside and tried to play a pass across the box to Brian Labone. Unfortunately, the pass was intercepted by Bobby Charlton, who drilled a shot just past the upright, much to the annoyance of Labby and my teammates. As I made my way back into position, Denis Law, the Manchester United and Scotland striker, gave me some advice.

'Don't you try and play football,' he said. Then, pointing over in the direction of George Best, he continued, 'You just keep kicking him!' Fortunately, I had the last laugh as we defeated them 1-0 thanks to a goal from David Johnson.

Towards the end of my Everton career I played in the 1977 League Cup final and replays before leaving the Blues in 1979 to play for Tulsa Rednecks in the USA.

In 1984 I was asked to return to Everton by Howard Kendall and Colin Harvey to take charge of the reserves before joining former Everton captain Mike Lyons at Grimsby Town in 1986.

Without hesitation I returned again just a year later when Howard moved to Spain to assist Colin Harvey. One of our first responsibilities was to take Everton, the newly crowned champions, on a tour of Australia and New Zealand to play exhibition matches. Before one game against Sydney FC there was a formal get-together of exiled Evertonians at a hotel in Sydney. Guest of honour at the presentation that day was none other than Mike Trebilcock, whose two goals had given such pleasure to the likes of me and thousands of Evertonians that famous day in May, 1966.

For guiding Everton to the league championship in 1987, Howard Kendall had deservedly been named Bell's Manager of the Year. Before the '87–88 season started I travelled up to Scotland with Howard to receive his award along with Adrian Heath, Peter Reid and Andy

Gray. The presentation took place in the afternoon, during which we enjoyed a few drinks. Afterwards we decided to go for a Chinese meal and a local suggested a restaurant by the docks. When we were waiting for a taxi at the hotel reception, Andy Gray, who was a great comedian as well as a great player, asked the receptionist if she had a stamp with the hotel's name on. When she said yes, he then asked her to stamp the hotel's name on my forehead. When she asked why, he explained that 'After a few drinks later he won't know where he's going so at least he can show his head to the taxi driver.' So she stamped my forehead and off we went.

In 1990, after 18 years as a player and a coach, my association with Everton Football Club ended. After leaving Everton, I spent time at Manchester City before enjoying 12 years at Blackburn Rovers.

After two knee replacements, in 2005 I had to leave coaching and became a scout, a role I still perform. Despite enjoying some good times at other clubs, if asked about my loyalty I tell people I couldn't be anything but an Evertonian; it's too much in me. Everton's my team and always will be.

Only 33 minutes of the 1966 Cup final remained for Everton to complete what seemed the impossible, yet that's what they did. Only a minute after Wednesday had taken a two-goal lead, Mike Trebilcock scored after Derek Temple's half-volley had been saved.

Five minutes later, Trebilcock doubled his and Everton's tally when he crashed home the equaliser past Wednesday's England keeper Ron Springett. The unbelievable was too much for two Everton supporters, who invaded the pitch to mob goal hero Trebilcock.

Roared on by their magnificent following there that day, Everton were now in the ascendancy as Wednesday, now very much on the back foot, clung on. Despite their efforts, with ten minutes remaining, Wednesday's resistance was finally broken when, after a mistake by Owls defender Gerry Young, Derek Temple took possession and sprinted towards the Wednesday goal. As Temple and Springett squared up one-on-one in this football 'duel', the keeper spat on his bare hands. Despite narrowing the angle, the England goalkeeper could do nothing to prevent Temple's perfectly timed and executed shot giving Everton their third goal and with it their third FA Cup final victory. In doing this, Ray Wilson became the only player to win both an FA Cup and World Cup winner's medal in the same season.

Despite the FA Cup achievement, Everton finished the 1965–66 season a disappointing 11th, their worst return in five years. Harry Catterick strengthened the side for the following season when he beat Leeds United to the signature of World Cup winner Alan Ball, who he signed from Blackpool for a record £110,000. In his first season with the Blues, when Everton travelled up to Newcastle United, Bally was determined to return with maximum points and a 'souvenir'.

Newcastle v Everton, 11 February 1967
Filthy McNasty by Colin Harvey

It was the year after Trebs popped up with those two goals at Wembley and we had the long journey up to Newcastle. We had just signed Alan Ball, who was fresh from being named man of the match in England's World Cup triumph. When Bally came to Everton, he had a mate called John who used to go to every single game Bally played. So, as usual, John was there the night we'd gone up to Newcastle. He even used to sleep on the floor in Bally's room, such was his dedication and loyalty.

Now Bally was a bit of a gambling man – he loved the horses, loved the dogs – even bowls. He just used to love any kind of bet. We were staying in a hotel called Gosforth Park, and as we pulled into the hotel we noticed there was a greyhound track next to it. Luckily, there was a meeting on that night so Bally (who was captain for this game) asked Harry Catterick if we could go to the dogs for a few hours. Harry said it was fine as long as we were all back on time. We were all delighted to get out of the hotel, no one more so than Bally.

That night the programme included a selling plate, a race which meant that the winner had to be sold. Bally had a bet on this dog – and I'll never forget the name: 'Filthy McNasty' – and lo and behold, it won. So Bally gave John about £50, and told him to buy it. He came back with this greyhound in his arms and said, 'What are we gonna do with it, Al?' Bally laughed and said that there was no way Harry Catterick would let him keep it in his room so he told John to take it home. So John had to take the dog back to Bolton. It was just John's luck that back in those days there were trains called 'milk trains' which stopped at pretty much every station on the way.

John actually looked after 'Filthy McNasty' until the day it died. We all called him John McNasty from then on and the name stuck. McNasty was more a fan of Bally than a fan of Everton – he idolised him. He was actually a Bolton fan originally who became an Evertonian just because of Bally. He didn't even get to see the Newcastle game in the end – it was unbelievable.

Alan Ball's luck didn't end at the race track. He also scored a penalty in the game at St James' Park, which Everton won 3-0.

Howard Kendall arrived for £80,000 from Preston in March 1967 and the season ended with Everton in sixth position.

Everton improved the following year, finishing fifth and making it to Wembley again. Unfortunately Everton could not match the heroics of two years earlier as they lost the final 1-0 to West Bromwich Albion despite being clear favourites. In the same year, Ken Loach directed The Golden Vision, a drama-documentary that focused on the lives of Everton supporters following the team home and away as well as real-life footage of Alex Young and behind-the-scenes events at Everton Football Club.

Everton's quality of football continued to improve, thanks largely to the skills and understanding of their midfield trio of Harvey, Kendall and Ball, referred to by fans as 'The Holy Trinity'. The team again progressed in the league, finishing third in the 1968–69 campaign as well as reaching the semi-final of the FA Cup.

However, the following season proved to be the pinnacle for this great side. They led for most of the 1969–70 season until just after Christmas when Leeds United took over at the top. After some indifferent form, Everton recovered and, thanks to Alan Whittle, who scored 15 goals in just 11 games, and Joe Royle's 23 goals, they lifted their seventh league title, finishing nine points ahead of second-placed Leeds.

Chelsea v Everton (source and date unknown)
The Shed

I lived in London in the sixties, so went to all the games there, when Everton came to visit.

My best mate was a Chelsea fan. This was back when Chelsea were a mid-table team and Everton were the best (West, Wright, Newton, Trinity, Morrissey, Whittle, Royle, Hurst *et al*). My mate had threatened for some time to take me to the The Shed, the most feared home end in London at the time. But I just laughed and told him with typical American bravado to 'Bring it on.' I was 13, I hurry to add, and don't think I am Clint Eastwood any more. But, at 13 you are indestructible.

So, when game day arrived, I pulled on my Everton scarf and hurried out the door. We walked to the bus stop and made it to Stamford Bridge. 'Where are our tickets?' I asked. He shot me a devilish grin and answered, 'In The Shed.' I laughed. 'You know, I am not taking my Everton scarf off,' I told him, although I honestly did not believe him.

We were then herded into The Shed, so now I knew I was deep in the heart of enemy territory, an Everton fan stuck in the middle of Chelsea's fanatical support, in the thick of cockney skinheads and bovver-boys. A mean-looking, close-cropped ginger-haired Chelsea fan with tattoos and bad teeth told me, 'You better hope your boys don't score today, mate.' I smiled and pushed my friend a few spots over.

They knew I was there, and they were not happy about it, which amused my friend no end. He was Jamaican, so stood out a little himself. He was keen to let them know that HE was a Chelsea fan and he had brought me there to convert me. I tried to say little, because my Yank accent had not yet mellowed into something that might have sounded more Irish by the time I left England.

The lads there took extra special glee in crushing the life out of me whenever the stand pushed forward on the terrace, but that was the worst I got. Maybe I was lucky it ended scoreless. I got a few punches on the way out, but my relative youth seems to have protected me. In any event, it helped make me a man, that never-ending process of facing one's fears that transcends puberty. I can still say, to this day, that I supported Everton at Stamford Bridge from deep inside The Shed, and lived to tell the tale.

When Everton visited Stamford Bridge the next two years, I made the ticket arrangements. Whoever said that wisdom doesn't visit 14-year olds?

The way the club look after their ex-players, the way the ex-players come back and talk so highly of the supporters and the club, the way their supporters treat their players, it's really one big circle here, it's never-ending and I think once you're in the circle, there's no way out of it, I think you're stuck with it and . . . I'm certainly in that circle now.

David Moyes, speaking on The Granada Programme, June 2003

The 1970s

While many thought this great side would go on to dominate English football, the next season Everton flopped to a very disappointing 14th and were beaten in the European Cup in the third round on away goals to Greek side Panathinaikos. Reaching the semi-final of the FA Cup proved little consolation, particularly as the defeat was at the hands of Liverpool.

In 1971, the 'Mersey millionaires' spent £1 million on improving Goodison Park when they built the current three-tier main stand and new powerful lights replaced the old floodlights, which took up residence at Prenton Park, Tranmere. In December of that year, after defeat to Derby County had dropped Everton to 18th, Harry Catterick shocked fans by selling crowd-favourite Alan Ball to Arsenal for £220,000 – Ball's second record transfer. Not long after this, Catterick suffered a heart attack whilst driving back from Sheffield. Although he was back in charge at Goodison in less than three months, he couldn't prevent Everton falling further behind when they ended '71–72 in 15th.

In April 1973, due to ill health, Catterick took on an executive role at the club and Everton finished the season 17th, their lowest league position since relegation in 1951.

The manager's role was taken by Billy Bingham, a former Everton player and Northern Ireland international, who had been part of the 1962–63 Championship winning side. Bingham's first purchase was Northern Ireland

ınal Dave Clements who, later that season, replaced Howard Kend-
ᴸ   e team. No longer a first-team regular, in February 1974 Kendall
moved to Birmingham City as Bob Latchford, a centre forward with a goalscoring reputation, travelled in the opposite direction in a part-exchange
deal worth £350,000.

Everton's fortunes improved as they finished 1973–74 in seventh,
with local lad Mike Lyons finishing as top scorer with nine goals.

In 1974, Colin Harvey, the last of the 'Holy Trinity', left for Sheffield
Wednesday while, in December, one of the great number 9s, Joe Royle, also
departed. Despite the loss of once key players, optimism was again high
amongst Everton fans who hoped for better things, particularly after the
arrival of Martin Dobson for £300,000 from Burnley – a British record for a
cash deal. With high expectations, fans continued to follow the Blues in their
thousands, whenever and wherever they played.

Plymouth Argyle v Everton. FA Cup 4th Round, 25 January 1975
Where There's a Will There's Away by Kenny Simpson

When my dad passed away in 1974 he left the few bob that he had in
a savings account to me and my brothers Joey, George and Billy. It
wasn't a great amount of money, probably enough for a little holiday,
but our Joey had a plan as to what to do with it. 'Let's invest it wisely,'
he said. 'Let's use the money to fly down to Plymouth to watch Everton in the FA Cup.' Without hesitation we agreed to his plan, but
none of us had ever flown before so we said 'OK Joey, you book it
then,' which he did. The only flight he could get was on a small plane
flying from Blackpool airport. So, on the day of the game, we took a
minibus from Liverpool to Blackpool to catch our flight.

We arrived at Blackpool airport which, in the 1970s, was spartan
to say the least. It was a bitterly cold January day with drops of snow
in the air as we made our way over to a tiny plane that was bobbing

up and down on the small stretch of runway. The 30 or so passengers nervously took their seats in preparation for take-off. It wasn't long before we were in the air, being tossed around and wondering if we had made the right decision. The flight took only about an hour, though it seemed much longer in the gale-force winds, but eventually we arrived at Exeter airport in one piece – just about.

In Exeter, relieved at being back on the ground, we got a lift in another minibus to Plymouth. As it was around noon we stopped off at a café en route for a bite to eat. As we were eating our lunch, still feeling fresh from our short, yet bumpy journey, we noticed several coaches carrying Everton supporters pulling into the car park. Fans leaving the coaches looked in a right state, like they'd just come off a jungle safari. As they entered the café I spotted a lad I worked with and he came over to where we were sat. 'God, you look fresh,' he said. We told him we'd flown down and he started yelling all over the café to the Everton supporters 'Hey, these lads have flown down.' Everton fans, many of whom were still half asleep, looked over at us with a mixture of disbelief, admiration and envy. 'What time did you set off then?' I asked.

'We set off at 10 o'clock,' he said. 'Last night!'

With a journey of 294 miles, Plymouth's Home Park is the furthest ground from Goodison Park and a difficult place to get to nowadays, let alone in 1975 when there weren't as many motorways or cars on the road. All of a sudden, the turbulence we encountered on our short flight paled into insignificance as we compared our contrasting travel experiences.

We left the café refreshed and continued to travel to Plymouth. All you could see on the journey from Exeter were coaches full of blue and white and these were by no means luxury coaches. After a few pints in Plymouth we made our way to the ground. Despite the horrendous journey experienced by those travelling by charabanc, Everton still brought thousands of fans – a full contingent that filled their allocation in the 38,000 crowd. In those days, Match of the Day was the only TV programme that showed football and its cameras covered only one or two main Saturday fixtures. Once inside Home Park we noticed that we were going to be on the television that evening, possibly because, as Plymouth were a division below us, the BBC saw it as a potential banana-skin for Everton, hoping for a cup upset for its viewers.

I can't remember too much about the game although an upset was never on the cards. Everton won the game comfortably. Martin Dobson had a great game and we won 3-1 thanks to a goal from Jim Pearson and a brace from Mike Lyons.

We headed back after the game to Exeter airport which, like Blackpool's, was very small. This time, there were two planes on the runway, one of which was ours which we headed towards. As we were stood on the runway outside the plane we noticed that the other plane had been chartered for the Everton players and staff. People from both flights were mingling together in the freezing conditions and I can remember vividly Martin Dobson and Bob Latchford on the tarmac strip outside their plane dressed in big, thick full-length sheepskin coats. We made our way over to where they were stood and for around 20 minutes talked about the game with them as well as Billy Bingham, the Everton manager. Even in the bitter conditions, rubbing shoulders with the players like this after the game made the whole experience worthwhile. It was more memorable than the match itself, as players in those days were held in such high esteem by supporters, just as much as they are today, if not more.

The players' plane was the first to leave so we wished them well before boarding our own flight. On the way back we reflected on the comfortable victory and began to predict who we might get in the next round draw that was to be made on the Monday.

Back in Liverpool around half-past nine, the four of us decided to finish the journey off by going for a few pints in the Everton Supporters' Club. We went to the club most Saturdays as our George lived on Goodison Road and it was a vibrant place to go after the game. When we arrived it was well before Match of the Day was due to start but just before it did, fans would leave the concert room downstairs and make their way upstairs to watch the selected games on the television. Sporting our blue and white scarves, during the broadcast we mentioned that we had been to the match that day. A buzz went round the club but nobody believed us, as many had relatives who had gone to Plymouth by coach, and were not expected back until around 3 or 4 o'clock on the Sunday morning. Eventually, as we explained our story, people began to believe us as it wasn't something your average supporter would do and not something either of us did again, which is a pity as it was a great way to watch a game.

As for my dad's approval, well, like his lads, he was a big Evertonian so I'm sure he'd have been made up with the way we invested his life's savings.

Throughout my career at Everton I have experienced a wonderful feeling of being accepted by the fans as 'one of the family' and the friendliness extended to me by all Liverpool people over the past ten years has been fantastic. I would like to believe that the passion that I have for Everton is the equal to that of all the magnificent fans.

Duncan Ferguson, Evertonfc.com, May 2006

Everton failed to keep the cup run going, losing at home in the fifth round to Fulham, although their league form was good. They finished 1974–75 in fourth; a position which gained them entry into the UEFA Cup.

Unfortunately, Everton once again failed to build on the progress made and were eliminated from the UEFA Cup in the first round and ended the season 11th.

At the end of the 1975–76 season, Bingham signed Andy King from Luton Town and, in December, brought in the crowd-pleasing Duncan McKenzie and midfielder Bruce Rioch. Despite these useful additions, in January 1977, as Everton sat in the bottom half of the table, Bingham was sacked.

On 30 January, Gordon Lee left the manager's job at Newcastle United to become successor to Billy Bingham as Everton's new boss. Within six weeks, Lee, a respected 'players' manager', was leading out Everton at Wembley for the League Cup final against Aston Villa. The game finished 0-0 so it was replayed at Hillsborough, the match ending this time 1-1. In the second replay, after leading the game, trailing, then equalising, Everton eventually lost the marathon tie 3-2, with only two minutes of extra time remaining at Old Trafford.

If this game was disappointing then the FA Cup semi-final at Maine Road against Liverpool proved even more so. Everton equalised on two occasions before Bryan Hamilton 'scored' the winner in the last minute, only to be deemed offside by controversial referee Clive Thomas. Despite protesting, Everton were forced into a second replay which they lost, again to a disputed decision. Despite the two long and exciting Cup runs, Everton failed to land any silverware that year and finished 1976–77 in ninth. Clive Thomas never offered an explanation for his bizarre decision, something which still rankles with many Blues.

The following season, Gordon Lee worked hard to resurrect Everton's fortunes. Performances improved and Everton began to play attractive football once again, finishing third, which guaranteed UEFA Cup qualification.

In the last game of the season, Everton entertained Chelsea at Goodison Park with Bob Latchford two goals short of reaching the 30-goal mark, a tally that would trigger a £10,000 payment from the Daily Express for anyone reaching this total. Everton led comfortably thanks to goals from Neil Robinson, Billy Wright, Mike Lyons, Martin Dobson and one from Latchford which put him on 29 league goals. Fans urged 'The Latch' to shoot at every opportunity and players looked for Bob every time there was a goal-scoring opportunity in an effort for him to finish the season as the league's leading scorer and scoop the prize. When Everton were awarded a penalty, regular penalty taker Martin Dobson gave Bob, who never took penalties, some advice before standing aside to let him take the spot kick. Everton fans rejoiced when Latchford sealed a 6-0 victory and the £10,000 prize, which the big centre forward shared with his teammates.

Everton v Chelsea, 29 April 1978
The Sky's the Limit by Mike Lyons

Immediately after the game we drove to Manchester airport from where we were due to fly off to Majorca for the team's end-of-season holiday. All the lads were there looking forward to the trip, as in professional football, because of the matches played over the busy Christmas period, you had to have your Christmas and New Year in the summer break. On many occasions over my career I had gone to bed on New Year's Eve at 8 o'clock only for the game to be called off the following day due to the weather. So for footballers this was the time to really relax before the pre-season and the hard work started again.

Anyway, we arrived at Manchester airport only to find our flight was delayed by more than three hours. With it being the end of season and our holiday, the players decided to relax and unwind by going for a few drinks. One drink led to another and as the drinks flowed, players started to enter into a bit of lively banter with each other as is the norm in most football teams' dressing rooms. The banter and the drinking even continued on to the flight as we became more and more drunk and more and more noisy.

Also at the airport were Johnny King's Runcorn FC, off on their end-of-season holiday to Ibiza. They had a big music system and both sets of players were singing and dancing to ease the boredom of the delay. On the plane I was sat next to Andy King while Mark Higgins was two rows in front of us. Shortly after taking our seats the plane took off and still the drinking and banter continued. As we were cruising around 30,000 feet over France, Andy King started to have a go at Mark Higgins' dad about his weight. Mark's dad John played for Bolton in the 1958 FA Cup final and had opened a pie factory after retiring from football. On hearing the insults directed at his dad, Higgy stood up from his seat and warned Kingy to lay off, saying 'You can say what you like about me but leave my family out of it.' Thinking Kingy would back off, Mark Higgins then sat down again. As soon as he did, Kingy jumped up out of his seat and started singing 'He's a big fat pig, he's a big fat pig.' On hearing this, Higgy lost his rag and launched backwards over the seats towards Kingy, who was in mid chorus.

Higgy grabbed hold of him, threw him on the floor, grabbed him by the throat and shouted, 'Right, me and you outside now!' Realising where we were, the rest of the lads, including Higgy and Kingy fell about laughing and that was the end of the matter. Typically it had to be Kingy, who was a real bubbly character and a great lad.

We bumped into the Runcorn team again, about four days later in Majorca after they had been deported from Ibiza!

Geoff Nulty signed for Everton from Newcastle in 1978 and was also a team-mate of Andy King's. Here, Geoff recalls his memories of Andy King.

Andy King was a great character, a laugh a minute who, along with the likes of Terry Darracott was a livewire and great lad to have in the dressing room. Although he was known for his great personality, Kingy also possessed remarkable ability as a footballer. He was an exceptionally skilful player who played in the 'hole' just behind Latchy. From there he would make his runs and was never picked up by opposition defenders. Before they knew it, he'd be in behind them, shimmy round the keeper and score. In my opinion, in that role he was the best in the First Division and should have been in the England squad every time it was picked – he was that good. Though I have many fond memories of Andy King, one story instantly springs to mind.

In 1980 my career was cut short after I suffered cruciate ligament damage in a match against Liverpool so I became a member of the Everton staff, assisting manager Gordon Lee. Also on the staff at the time was Colin Harvey, who was reserve team coach, and Harry Cooke. As chief scout, Harry was well respected and was often entrusted to buy players for small fees without the manager's authorisation. Around this time, Harry had brought over a lad from Northern Ireland for a small fee who he felt was a good prospect. He was in the mould of Johnny Morrissey, a sturdy outside right who was also quick and quite aggressive. Harry gave this brief to Colin Harvey so the lad was put into the reserves to see how he performed.

The following day, after the Central League game, Colin came upstairs at Goodison to meet with the other coaches. When he arrived he said to Harry Cooke, 'Hey, that lad, you'll never believe what happened to him last night.' And he told the story of the game.

'During the first half, the lad was playing on the right-hand side, working up and down the touchline close to us. We were surprised because he was just non-existent. He wouldn't go past the player or put his foot in and when he went into a challenge with the full-back he would pick him straight up before apologising.' So, at half-time Colin had a word with him, saying, 'Come on son, show yourself a bit more, you've got to start putting your foot in a bit more and get into the game.'

On hearing this, the young lad looked up at Colin and said 'I'm sorry, I can't do that. I can't hurt him.'

Colin looked puzzled and replied 'But that's your game, put your foot in and make your presence felt.'

'No,' he said. 'When I was on the boat on the way over here I had a dream and in the dream the Lord said to me I must change my ways and not hurt anyone any more. I'm a reformed character now.'

At this point Colin didn't know what to say as the dressing room fell silent and all eyes turned in the young boy's direction. Lads, including Andy King, who was having a run-out in the game to regain match fitness after returning from injury, looked on in disbelief, not knowing whether to laugh or cry. Colin then said, 'Look, son, if you want to make a career of this and make the first team in the near future then that's what you'll have to do.'

'That's the other thing,' he said. 'In my dream the Lord also said to me that the world was going to end next year.' After a brief pause of deadly silence, nobody knowing what to say, Kingy popped up and in his own comical way shouted, 'Yeah, we know son, that's why you've only been given a 12-month contract!' Typical Kingy!

Two years after Everton's last, albeit brief, European venture, fans dusted the cobwebs from their passports and embarked on another overseas Blue excursion, though not all foreign visits proved to be plain sailing.

Dukla Prague v Everton, UEFA Cup 2nd leg, 1 November 1978
The Alternative Hitchhiker's Guide to Europe by Steve Bird

In 1978 I was 20 and my brother Mark was 18. One Sunday afternoon we were drinking in our local, The Falstaff in Childwall, with a few of the lads, talking about Everton's forthcoming UEFA Cup second round second leg on the following Wednesday away at Dukla Prague. Everton had won the first leg at Goodison 2-1 thanks to goals from Bob Latchford and Andy King so the tie was finely balanced. Suddenly a bet with the lads was offered that we would never make it. So I said 'Right, we'll go!' The lads questioned how we were going to get there with such short notice saying we wouldn't have enough time to get on to the club tour. 'We won't go on the club tour,' I said. 'We'll make our own way.'

'How are you gonna do that?' they asked.

'Well, we'll start today,' and with that Mark and I went home to our house that was about a hundred yards away, got two Adidas bags, threw a load of gear in and got on the 79A bus to the Fiveways, walked over to The Rocket and put out our thumbs. The only bit of research I had done prior to this moment was that I knew that if you wanted to get into Czechoslovakia you had to have a visa. So the plan was to hitchhike to London first in order to go to the Czech embassy to get a visa.

Things started well as we got a lift at The Rocket straight away and were dropped off at Burtonwood services. However, after the promising start the lifts dried up and nine hours later we were still at Burtonwood. By this time our Mark seemed like he was coming down with hypothermia and started asking to go home. 'No,' I said. 'We're gonna do this, prove these fellas wrong and prove to them that it can be done.'

Eventually we hitched a few lifts and ended up spending the Sunday night sleeping rough on trolleys at King's Cross station. We woke up early on the Monday morning and made our way on the tube across London to the Czech embassy. At the embassy we went straight in, paid a few quid, got our visas stamped and were good to go. The only problem was that the embassy had told us that hitchhiking was illegal in Czechoslovakia. In my mind I had a rough geographical idea where Prague was and worked out that the best way to get around this was to get to the nearest point close to Prague, which was probably Nuremberg, Germany. So off we went. We hitched down to Dover, paid to get on to the ferry and started hitching again at Calais.

The first day was quite slow. Eventually we got to Belgium and got our heads down for the night. Mark had a sleeping bag but I had to sleep in a telephone box. In the morning I was woken by a trucker wanting to make a call, so got up and carried on hitching. We managed to get a lift from Brussels to Liège from a Belgian trucker. His English wasn't very good and it seemed a bit strange because every time we passed a layby he had to stop as if he was tired and needed a rest. Because it was late he said we could stop at his, which we did. We were starving and he started to cook us some ravioli and cheese. When he went into the kitchen I said 'Hey, look at that.' He was actually recording what we were saying on a tape recorder. I said, 'This is weird, we've gotta get out of here.' But we were both starving so had to hang on.

Thankfully nothing happened and in the morning he dropped us off at Aachen on the Dutch border. We hitchhiked through there, and from Frankfurt to Nuremberg. When we got to Nuremberg station our train to Prague wasn't set to leave for another seven hours. So to kill some time we went on the ale. I liked a pint and started walloping it but my brother was starting to worry about the money. 'We've got to get back on this money as well, remember,' he said. So I devised a plan to get us some quick money.

We went down to the toilets at the station where a lot of what looked like rent boys were. My brother was a good-looking New Romantic type with striking long blonde hair at the front (although now he's bald!). The plan was that he would go to the toilets and if anyone showed an interest in him, he would let me know and I would give them a hard time to get some money. Extortion I know, but when you're abroad you've got to think on your feet. It wasn't long before a couple of lads tried it on so I rushed over, saying, 'Hey, what's going on, give us 20 Marks or we're going to the police.'

This was working well and we managed to get about 40 Marks and I went back up for another drink. At the bar a Belgian man heard I was English and started to talk about the war. He began to buy me drinks but they weren't beers, they were like schnapps, a drink called un gebrau. I started knocking them back in one and he would get in another, raising his glass before toasting 'Vinston Churchill!'

After drinking a good few of these I was well on my way to being bladdered and had forgotten my brother, who I had left down in the toilets. The next thing I knew, our Mark flew up the stairs, screaming 'Where have you been? I've had loads of fellas trying it on!'

Eventually he calmed down and we boarded our train. I remember it being really warm. There was no air conditioning so I lay flat out in a small compartment stripped to the waist. The next thing I knew I was being woken by Czech border guards about 3 o'clock in the morning. One of them was a woman who looked like a shot putter, except her beard was better than Geoff Capes's. She slapped me before telling me to get my shirt on. Welcome to Czechoslovakia!

We finally reached Prague but had no tickets for the match so headed off in search of the hotel where the players were staying. We found it, went in and started chatting to a few of them. Geoff Nulty sorted us out with tickets and, not only did he do that, he also bought us a meal because we'd hitched all the way over.

Delighted at getting to Prague and securing tickets, we made our way to the game. There were 35,000 fans there, a lot of whom were Czech Army dressed in their uniforms – Dukla Prague had a big army following. At 0-0, things were going fairly well until the 80th minute when Dave Thomas tried to clear a ball from just outside his own box and it fell to a player called Gajdusek, who scored.

Typically the game finished 1-0 and we were out of Europe – a normal away trip really. After the match we were faced with another three days of hitchhiking. I thought, 'I don't fancy this' and, having an Everton tracksuit on tried to get into the dressing room. As I looked like an Everton official, they just let us straight in. Inside we started to tell our story to Mike Lyons. 'We've got to hitchhike for another three days to get back, Mike,' I said.

Mike Lyons was humbled by our story. 'You've got to hitchhike all the way back after watching that?' he said. 'Oh no, you're not doing that,' and he called over Ralph Williams who was Everton's Commercial Manager. 'Ralph,' he said, 'these lads are coming back on the plane with us. They hitchhiked all the way here and we let them down so they are coming back with us.'

The next thing we knew we were on the players' coach going to Prague airport. At the airport we tried to exchange the Czech currency we had left over at the bureau de change as we had about 40 quid's worth left. Unfortunately, being an Eastern European country they were more interested in western currency so wouldn't exchange our money. Stuck with 40 quid's worth of Krona we had no option but to spend it at the bar so ended up buying four trays of beer. We started sharing the lagers with the players and a few of them were getting a taste for it, so much so that Everton's manager Gordon Lee came over and asked us not to give them any more.

By the time I got on to the plane I'd drunk that much I thought I was the pilot, flying the plane from the back seat. As it was taking off down the runway I was going mad, shouting, 'Neeeoww,' and had to be restrained.

The flight arrived back at Liverpool airport and we made our way back to The Falstaff to claim our money from the bet. We took a programme as evidence and collected our winnings, which I think was a fiver, although we had spent about three hundred quid getting there! About a month later details of our epic journey were published in the Everton programme.

After losing another European fixture on away goals, Everton's focus was now to make progress in Division One. But would a former crowd favourite halt Everton's progress?

The Everton fans are a special breed who have a really strong relationship with the club. They used to roar my name. For a foreign player, that's special. We went to Anderlecht once and you should have seen how many travelled.

Thomas Gravesen, Evertonfc.com, May 2005

Everton v Chelsea, 11 November 1978
The Entertainer by Martin Dobson

My first experience of Everton and its magnificent supporters was when I watched the 1966 FA Cup final. I was 18 and had just signed for Bolton Wanderers. I can remember watching the game on TV with my dad and at 2-0 down thinking it was all over for Everton. But my dad, who was a quiet man, said 'They just need a break. If they get one back, something might happen.'

My dad was right and I remember Eddie Cavanagh running on to the pitch after Everton scored the winner. You could see by his expression how much Everton meant to him. His celebratory run and emotions encompassed everything the club signified for him and the other supporters there that day. Everton's ability to overturn a 2-0 deficit was, of course, largely due to the efforts of the players but I believe it was a collective effort and Everton won the Cup that day helped by the crowd.

I supported Everton that day not knowing that several years later I would be joining them for a record fee. The events of 1966 were at the back of my mind when Billy Bingham asked me to sign, which I did without hesitation.

When I played for Everton I always felt supported by the fans and enjoyed it when the Gwladys Street would sing 'Martin Dobbo, Martin Dobbo, Allo, Allo.'

One of my highlights as an Everton player came in the derby match at Goodison in October 1978. Mike Lyons, the captain, was injured so as vice-captain I stepped up to skipper the side. Walking out at Goodison that afternoon against my opposite captain Kenny Dalglish was a proud moment – something I'll never forget. As Kenny and I led our teams up the steps we were met by a huge roar, the like of which I'd never heard before.

I remember being met by this wall of sound as we ran out on to the field and thinking 'Wow, what a noise!' It was deafening and when I heard it I thought 'We can't let them down' and thankfully we didn't, thanks to Andy King's magnificent drive. Though I have many fond memories of Everton supporters, it was the game at Goodison against Chelsea a month later that sticks out in my mind as being particularly unusual, something which I believe makes Everton fans unique.

Everton's manager at the time was Gordon Lee and we were in second place, having a decent run in the league. I liked Gordon as he was straight and honest. He had a strong work ethic and produced a hard-working, well-organised team. Not only that, he also got us play-ing attractive, successful football.

But during his time at Goodison Park he had a problem with Duncan McKenzie as he often wanted more effort from him. Duncan was a character and still is. I saw Duncan at a Foundation dinner recently and he was still the same; a laugh a minute. He was great in the dressing room. Every team needs somebody to put a smile on faces when a result has gone the wrong way. Duncan had a great personality and philosophy towards football and life. Nothing seemed to get him down. He was an extrovert. He could even jump over a Mini Cooper and throw a golf ball the length of the pitch.

All Evertonians loved the way Duncan played the game – trying different things in an effort to create or score a goal. Who can ever forget the televised match against Stoke City when he ran the show? Entertainer personified. He was capable of producing a bit of magic that could change a game and he had a special relationship with the fans who wanted to win and win in an entertaining way.

This was illustrated in the FA Cup semi-final against Liverpool the previous year. On a rain-soaked, muddy Maine Road, his great balance helped him glide over the pitch that day and score as well. Duncan epitomised what Evertonians wanted to see and, as a result, they loved him, and he loved them.

But still Gordon wasn't totally convinced and eventually sold Duncan to Chelsea despite Duncan not wanting to leave.

The fixtures soon brought us together at Goodison Park and during the game against Chelsea that November day the strangest thing happened. I had never experienced it before and never have since.

Duncan scored for Chelsea and the 38,000 plus supporters at Goodison rose to acclaim the goal from the former crowd favourite. I remember running back to the halfway line for the kick-off and looking at Andy King. Our expressions were a picture. 'What's all that about, Dobbo?' said Kingy. 'We're 1-0 down and the fans have gone berserk!'

It just showed how the fans appreciated the way Duncan played the game. To receive an ovation like that from opposition supporters was remarkable – even more so when you consider that Duncan played only 48 games for Everton.

It all worked out fine in the end for us that day, though. It was particularly pleasing for me because after going behind again, 2-1, I got on the end of two Dave Thomas crosses to head in at the far past, to win the game 3-2.

I saw Duncan in the players' room afterwards and he was chuffed to bits with the reception he'd received from the Goodison faithful. And, deep down, I don't think Duncan was too disappointed that we went away with maximum points.

With regards to individual fans I remember one in particular.

Bob Latchford,, Jim Pearson, John Connolly and I lived in the Formby/ Southport area and we used to travel in for training and matches together. On our way home after away games we would drop in to the local pub. The landlord of our local, Sid, was an avid Evertonian with a great personality who was always cracking jokes.

After beating Birmingham at St Andrew's we stopped off for one and outside the pub was a notice saying:

'Pie and a pint and a friendly word.'

We went in, got the round in but, despite Everton's victory, Sid was in a right stroppy mood – not a word for the cat.

So I said, 'Hey up, Sid, what's up mate? Outside it says – a pie and a pint and a friendly word. Where's the friendly word?'

Quick as a flash he came straight back and said to me,

'Don't eat the pies, Dobbo!' then cracked up laughing.

He'd done us up like a kipper.

I was sad to have to leave Everton in 1979 but I try and get back there whenever I can as it's a special club with special fans.

For the first time in many years, Gordon Lee brought stability back to Goodison Park when Everton finished the 1978–79 season in fourth. Consistency in the league would also see the club in Europe for the second successive season, although again they disappointed fans by being eliminated from the UEFA Cup in the first round.

Despite another FA Cup semi-final appearance in 1980, Everton ended the new decade in 19th. Not sure as to when Everton would be back in Europe, fans began to travel to pre-season European friendlies to get the most out of their passports before their ten-year validity expired.

It's always a great pleasure for me to come to Goodison because I usually get booed when I play away from home! I suppose that's normal in football, but when I come back here I feel incredibly emotional, especially when I take corners. I really appreciate it and because of it, I will always have a special place in my heart for the Everton supporters for the rest of my life.

Paulo di Canio, Evertonfc.com, January 2004

The 1980s

Pre-season tour to Marbella, 1980
Foreign Currency by Mick Upfield

The summer pre-season tour of 1980 was made public by Everton in early June and included a four-team tournament in Marbella. As flights to that part of Spain were not cheap, I arranged to meet up with friends – Gary Paterson, Dave Vickers and Terry McKernan – one Friday night in London to decide the best way to get there. Late in the day another friend, Kenny Evans, expressed an interest and the group of five was complete.

We met up in Snows, a tourist 'cockney style' establishment in Leicester Square, and options were discussed. The preferred choice was a flight, but at that time I had a major fear of flying and managed to convince them that an overland adventure was the way to go. Inter-Rail offered fares of around £150, which at the time was very expensive, so we opted for a coach to Barcelona and then a hire car to Marbella. Little did we know what we had let ourselves in for.

It was a sunny morning in late July when we left for Victoria coach station and the excitement was overwhelming. This soon turned to a little bit of uneasiness when we saw the coach that we had booked to travel on. Julia Coaches! It had a ring to it for all the wrong reasons.

A few weeks before one of these scheduled long-distance coaches had crashed and there had been fatalities. Ah well, in for a penny (well £75), in for a peseta. If we didn't get on we wouldn't get to Barcelona.

The journey started off uneventfully but it was soon made obvious to us that we were the odd ones out on the bus. Most of the other passengers were Spanish folk returning home for holidays. We were the five British lads laughing and joking at the back of the coach, knocking back our carry-out. Needless to say what goes in as liquid usually has to come out again and we must have made a pretty sight relieving ourselves in a line in the car park at the white cliffs at Dover.

A short hop across the Channel spent in the bar didn't help the situation either and the rest of the journey was spent desperately anticipating the next scheduled toilet stop.

As evening fell and darkness came we circumnavigated the Paris Périphérique and an eerie silence settled as people drifted into slumber. Not the Evertonians; oh no, we were getting to grips with our duty frees purchased from the ferry and managed to gather together the rest (well two) of the Brits for an impromptu party on the back seats. Interestingly enough, one of the new Brits was a Brummie lass who was travelling to Barcelona to work as a belly dancer! That impressed us I can tell you. The journey seemed to go on and on and the Spaniards were getting more upset that we needed so many stops to get rid of the liquid.

On arrival in Barcelona, weary, hungry and with not a clue where we were supposed to pick up the car we set ourselves the task of getting some lunch. As with previous foreign trips, none of us could speak the lingo, so we improvised by communicating with a Spanish waiter (no, he wasn't fat and did not suffer from kidney stones) by using very slow English and some body popping sign language, to order a bowl of hot tomato soup each.

Half an hour later, we finished our glasses of cold tomato juice, picked up our hire car and set off to find the campsite that would be our home while in Benidorm.

It was situated on the outskirts of the resort and we realised we had to take a bus into the centre. Kenny was lagging behind, complaining that he felt crap. Showing absolutely no sympathy, we walked on. As we stood at the bus stop, we watched in amazement as Kenny, on the other side of the road, produced an arc of orangecoloured spew. This became known as the 'Fanta Fountain' and was not the last time it came up on the trip, as it were.

After enjoying a couple of nights out in Benidorm, we travelled on to Malaga. In the town we stopped at traffic lights and noticed a car, containing a few youths, pull up alongside. They shouted what appeared to be some insult that included 'Barcelona Bastardo' or something like that. Unmoved, we wound down the windows and gave a loud cry of 'EV-ER-TON' and they accelerated away. We had not done anything to offend them before the outburst and can only think they thought we were from Barcelona as we had Barcelona number plates. Not long after this we arrived in Torremolinos, quickly found some accommodation and made our way to the night life.

Out on the town, we met up with some fellow ESCLA members (Everton Supporters Club London Area) and arranged a lift on their coach to the first match against Castilla on the Thursday in Marbella, some thirtyodd miles away. Until then it was party time. The booze and rich food soon took their toll. Terry and Dave went down with food poisoning the day of the game and like Kenny received no sympathy from the remaining three of us. We blamed any inconsistent toilet habits on the beer and continued to knock them back. Terry and Dave managed to get some Immodium-type concoction from the local doctor, which was supposed to act like a temporary cork. This it duly did . . . sort of.

Talking of toilet habits; that afternoon Gary found himself without a toilet roll in a bar toilet near the beach and had to resort to using 100 peseta notes. Not to be out of pocket, he duly washed them in the sea and dried them on the sand before returning to the same bar to spend them. Luckily for us we never received a 100 pesetas note in our change after that.

The time to catch the coach came and, after much deliberation, Terry and Dave decided to risk it and travel. We arrived near the stadium in Marbella and quickly took over the local hostelry. After a couple of beers, Terry Underwood, one of the ESCLA lads, decided that a trip to the ground for a look at the stadium was in order. We all agreed and set off to the main entrance where we were greeted by an armed security guard, pretty much like the corps of commission-aires that they have at Goodison, but with guns. A few of the lads had replica tops on, and, as we stood in an orderly queue outside the main door, I flashed my ESCLA Card.

The card was officiallooking and incorporated a club crest. Unbe-lievably, the guard waved us in and showed us to the dressing rooms. We were gobsmacked but decided that this was an opportunity not to be missed. We went into what was akin to a 'Corpy' Sunday League dress-ing room and made out we were preparing for the match. The laugh-ing was infectious and some started doing warm-ups, which didn't help.

We were finally rumbled about ten minutes later, but the Marbella officials took it in good humour. We even picked up some match post-ers as souvenirs before making our way back to the bar.

Kick-off came and we were outplayed by Castilla, a feeder club for Real Madrid who would put West Ham out of the Cup Winners' Cup later that year. A debut Everton goal for a young Graeme Sharp, laid on by Asa Hartford, was wiped out by three of theirs and the match finished in a 3-1 defeat at about 12.15 a.m. The match kicked off on a Thursday and finished on a Friday. That must have been a first.

After the match we made our way back to the coach and set off along the coast road to Torremolinos. About three miles out of town, the Immodium-cork finally gave way and Terry had to find sanctu-ary behind an advertising hoarding by the side of the road. He reap-peared a couple minutes later looking very pale and minus his match souvenir poster. He looked awful.

Terry and Dave did not recover enough to make the play-off against Portuguese side Belenenses. We decided that it would be better for them to claim a flight back to Britain on their insurance and made the necessary arrangements. A quick reply from their insurers had them booked on a flight the following Monday, which meant they would have a couple of nights extra in the apartment. We all chipped in and paid the extra for them.

The time came to set off to Marbella for the second match so we loaded up the car and drove to the ground. Arriving early, we wandered around and, as I was driving, avoided the bars. We received the same friendly welcome as we had two days earlier, though we did not try any stunts regarding entry to the ground. The Everton team bus arrived not long after us and we chatted to the players and had pictures taken. We even managed to get Gordon Lee to don a sombrero and pose for us. It has never ceased to amaze me how, over the years, players at Everton have always been approachable. There is nothing that is too much trouble for them and they always give fans the time of day and appear interested in them.

Inside the ground, more pictures with the players were taken and I managed to get one with Bob Latchford which is still on my office wall today. I once spent a late night after Brian Labone's funeral in the Holiday Inn bar with Bob and he explained over a couple of beers how Everton were the unluckiest team in the '70s. Apart from being Champions in 1970, we had bad luck for the rest of it including that Brian Hamilton winner that was wiped out by Clive 'the bastard book' Thomas, three games against Villa in the League Cup, and narrow European exits against Panathinaikos, Dukla Prague and Feyenoord. Needless to say, he was right.

Everton won the match against Belenenses 4-1 and we drove off into the night leaving the bright Costa lights behind us. We anticipated about eight hours' total driving time to get back to Barcelona.

During a short stop to fix a puncture, and knowing that Gary was a bit uneasy about snakes, it wasn't long before the hissing started.

'I wouldn't stand there, Gary . . . snakes in the grass up here,' which forced Gary out on to the tarmac. We found it highly amusing; well at least for a minute or so, as we just couldn't get the wheel brace to shift the hubcap. Gary, who had been the most inventive with pesetas during the trip, suggested using coins. I managed to get one of the bigger coins under the hubcap, moving it a little, and then Kenny shifted it. After a couple of attempts, the hubcap went on its merry way down the road. On seeing this, we jumped up and down and hugged each other as if we had won the Cup. If anyone had seen us they would have sectioned us as lunatics. Three grown men stood, hugging and cheering on a deserted road halfway up a Spanish mountain in the early hours of the morning? Sheer ecstasy.

We made it back to Barcelona in good time, visited the Nou Camp, watched a training session, upset the goalkeeping coaching staff by cheering as goals went in and still caught the coach.

On the outward journey, we had learned that it was not wise to drink too much as toilet stops were at a premium and, besides, we were so knackered that we slept for most of it.

Back on home soil, we vowed never to do it again. But, thirty years on, it does seem very appealing.

Pre-season Tour, 1980 or 1981
Sisters and Blisters by Pat Cooney

I began 'properly' following the Blues in about 1976–77 and started going home and away. My sister and I were befriended by a group of women from the Highfield Street area, ex Tate and Lyle workers and characters to say the least. I was about 14 and they looked after me, but to be honest I never really felt in any danger on those away trips. All I can remember is laughing through that era.

The pre-season tour must have been either the summer of '80 or '81. I know we'd either just signed, or not long signed, a young, slim Graeme Sharp. (A bit different now!) A group of us, girls and fellas aged between late teens and early twenties, made the journey by train and boat from Liverpool to Southern Spain. I think the tournament was either in Malaga or Marbella but we stayed in Torremolinos. We'd gone on the train from Liverpool to London, got across London, took another train to Dover followed by a really rough crossing to France. Then, finally, we hopped on to another train to Paris. All in all, the journey was pretty horrible: packed trains, heat, cramped conditions, not to mention French people!

I think it must have been in Paris that we got off and stretched our legs on the platform. Some of the lads saw that the first class carriages were empty, and as the ticket inspectors had already been around decided to bunk in and take a chance – after all, what's the worst that could happen? The more cowardly amongst us stayed put. I think the next stop was San Sebastian in northern Spain, where we were searched by police with dogs that looked like wolves. I think it was the quietest we'd been all journey. Anyway, we weren't allowed off the train so we continued on and I think it was in Madrid we discovered that some of the lads were missing. (Like I said, it was an epic journey – the things you do for the Blues!) Anyway, we eventually got to Torremolinos and there was still no sign of them. They eventually turned up a day or so later. Their part of the train had split from ours and they ended up in Lourdes of all places!

That trip is also personally memorable for the fact that I fell asleep under a parasol, after forgetting the sun cream. My feet weren't under the shade and later that night, as we sat in a pavement cafe, I began to feel really hot, and looked down to see a huge blister appearing on my ankle. So what do you do? You go home and burst it of course. Shit! The next morning I woke up with pus oozing from this open wound. I couldn't put my foot flat on the floor and ended up going to the game wearing one flip flop and one three-inch heeled mule! The arena was a concrete dump somewhere in the Malaga region.

I'm pretty sure Bob Latchford (my hero) was with us and I jumped over the small wall to get a picture, only to discover there was about a five-foot drop on the other side! The pain was unbearable. My mates then had the bright idea of asking Jim McGregor (the physio at the time) to have a look at it. Jim was a star – he had a quick look and invited me in to dress my foot. We hobbled round to the dressing room, knocked and I remember him opening the dressing room door and a half naked Asa Hartford, lying on the treatment table, hastily reaching for something to cover his modesty. Those were the days!!

The following year was equally disappointing and, towards the end of the 1980–81 season, with Everton languishing in 15th, Gordon Lee was sacked.

His replacement was former Championship winner Howard Kendall, the player-manager at Blackburn Rovers, who took over in May 1981. Excited at the arrival of their former favourite, fans continued to follow Everton home and away – some were even prepared to change their identities.

Everton are a bigger club than Liverpool. Everywhere you go on Merseyside you bump into Everton supporters.

Graeme Souness

Ipswich Town v Everton, 11 December 1982
Nothing to Report by Kenny Evans

Back in the days when you could roll up and buy tickets for the game, Paul McBride and I arrived at Ipswich Town's box office nice and early looking to buy two tickets. As these were hooligan-fuelled days, and people were getting wise to tricks of all sorts in gaining entry to parts of the ground they shouldn't be in, we decided to toss to see who would go up to the counter. I lost, so in my best 'yokel' accent I ordered two tickets. 'Where for?' came the reply . . . bugger! 'Erm, the best you have, young lady.'

'That'll be £12 each.'

With tickets in hand, I thought we'd just have to go easy on the ale to avoid being detected. Easier said than done though, eh?

Once inside, we found our seats and that the joke was firmly on us. Best seats in the house? Yes, they were on the halfway line, but stuck right in front of us was a pillar. Great view, eh? I'm sure the girl in the ticket office had seen right through my disguise. Perhaps the piece of straw in the corner of my mouth was a dead give away.

Not to be outdone, we realised that to our left, across the aisle, was the press box.

Shortly after kick-off, the box had two new additions. Having no accreditation, we were amazed we slotted in. It must have been our haggard, weather-beaten looks that made us pass for journalists; either that or they couldn't be bothered. I think it was probably the latter as there were plenty of seats, or maybe it was down to Everton not being 'top drawer' at the time.

Trying to blend in and look like we knew what we were doing, we proceeded to switch on the strip light underneath the writing shelf, but alas, we had no phone to plug in. I think we managed a ball-point pen between us but with nothing to write on. Journos? Us? Not a chance. But we had blagged our way into some good seats without as much as a hat with a card stuffed in the ribbon.

Everton were languishing in mid-table mediocrity and even from our new vantage point the game was a dreary affair – until the last ten minutes or so. A goal from Kevin Richardson brought two 'reporters' jumping for joy attracting strange looks from those inside and outside the press box. Some of the tabloids' finest looked on as if to say 'Decorum, dear boys, remember where you are.' Assuming our cover had been blown we sat back down and thought 'Ah well, this is where we get ejected by some security guard or other.' But nothing happened, and we stayed to witness the increasing tension as Ipswich pressed for an equaliser.

In the last few minutes of the game, a cross came over from the left and Kevin Sheedy scored what was to be our eventual winner. The two pseudo journos were up and dancing again amid glum faces and seasoned Fleet Street hacks. We didn't give a toss. The Blues had won and that was all that mattered – you know the feeling.

The final whistle was blown and, without a sentence written or single call made, our time in the press box came to an end. A real-life journo, whose knowledge of Everton was somewhat limited, approached us and asked who crossed the ball for Everton's second goal. Always happy to exchange some information with a fellow reporter, quick as a flash we replied 'Terry Curran.'

Unknown to us, behind us, and studying our behaviour during the game, was a reporter who must have been from the Echo or Daily Post. On gathering his notes together, he said, 'That's how it should be in the Press Box every f**kin' week!' I reckon he was right but, surprisingly, no offers of employment ever came our way.

West Ham v Everton, 2 January 1982
Czech Please by Frank Stafford

My first Everton match was against Fulham at Goodison Park in 1963, the year we won the league championship. I went to the game with my granddad because my dad, who was a Red, worked away from home. My granddad seized the opportunity to give me a proper education, which, I'm glad to say, he did. After the 4-1 victory I went to many matches both home and away with my granddad until I was old enough to go to every game with my mates.

In 1982, we were drawn against West Ham United at Upton Park in the third round of the FA Cup. I travelled down to London with three other lads from Cantril Farm, Huyton – my uncle David Dale, Danny Ryan and an old fella called Victor. My uncle Dave had a few bob and would take us to matches in his flash car. When we would get to the game, Danny and myself would go for a few pints while Dave and Victor would have a coffee. Old Vic was an ill man, who suffered with heart problems, and Everton was his life. He would go to the match with his old Army haversack, flask of coffee and tablets for his heart condition. Although only in his sixties, old Vic was dying. He suffered with heart problems for years and I think following Everton kept him alive. The Blues gave him something to live for.

We arrived early but only David and Victor had tickets so we left them to search for a way to see the game. After making several attempts, a West Ham supporter said our best bet was probably to ask at the West Ham Supporters Club so off we went, a last-ditch attempt to get tickets. We arrived at the club, which was just next to the ground, around 2 o'clock and knocked on the door. Danny had a really thick Scouse accent, spoke about a hundred miles an hour and was difficult to understand, even for people who knew him well. When a fella answered the door Danny was in pole position. Excited at the prospect of getting a ticket for the match, quick as a flash he blurted out 'Any chance of a ticket there, lad?' However, it probably sounded more like 'Enychanza verticker derlad?' The bloke paused for a moment then looked at him as if to say 'What did you say?'

Then, speaking slowly, a man behind us asked, 'Oh, are you the Czechoslovakian people?' to which Danny just nodded with a puzzled look on his face. 'Come with me,' he said and took us inside and to the bar where he instructed the barmaid to serve us a complimentary drink. He went behind the bar and returned with a brown envelope containing two tickets for the match. He handed them over, saying, 'I hope you have an enjoyable afternoon.'

He then told the barmaid to give us anything we wanted before leaving us alone. We drank as much as we could in 45 minutes and set off for the match. The lad that had given us the tickets even shook our hands as we left and wished us well.

When we got inside the ground we found our seats were right in among the West Ham fans as the tickets were intended for Czechoslovakian people who obviously supported The Hammers.

Everton scored early on through Peter Eastoe and we jumped up out of our seats. The West Ham fans sitting around us resembled something from The Krays with their Abercrombies and big cigars. They were all shouting abuse at us, telling us to 'Sit down you scouse gits' but it never stopped us. All in all though, a great, free afternoon spoiled only by the fact we lost the match 2-1.

Several years later, in the summer of 1986, a gang of us, including Danny, were on holiday in Spain. One day on the beach, one of the lads saw someone he thought was an Everton coach. He turned and asked, 'Hey Frank, is that Mick Heaton?' I looked at the person he pointed at but thought it wasn't him as this fella had a moustache and Mick Heaton never did. Then Danny noticed he had an Everton towel on his sunbed and said, 'Yeah it must be him'. Danny waited until he walked past and asked, 'Have you finished with that sunbed, mate?'

The bloke replied, 'Yeah, help yourself mate.' Danny then shouted, 'Are we selling that Gary Stevens then or what?' in reference to the fact that it was Gary Stevens who was at fault for one of the goals in the '86 cup final defeat to Liverpool. 'If it was up to me I'd sell him tomorrow,' came the reply, so it obviously was Mick Heaton.

Mick went for a drink in a bar further along the beach so we followed him. We ended up drinking together every night after that and got on well with Mick, so much so that at the end of the holiday he gave me Gary Lineker's '86 cup final shirt and gave Peter Reid's to Danny.

After the holiday we kept in touch with him and became good friends. He was very generous and would get us tickets for away games. But he left the Blues in 1987 in search of a new challenge. He became manager of non-league Workington Town and we would go and watch them if Everton weren't playing.

In 1990 Everton played Manchester City at Maine Road. Howard Kendall was in charge of City so Mick was able to get us tickets. After the match, which we lost 1-0, we were invited into Howard Kendall's office for a drink. In the office Danny and I were drinking with Mick, Colin Harvey, Howard Kendall and some other lads from Liverpool. Howard cracked open a crate of Lamot Pils lager for us and after downing a few bottles, Danny told everyone the story of our trip to West Ham when they thought we were Czechoslovakians. After hearing the story they all burst out laughing and Howard wiped away the tears from his eyes before saying, 'Only Evertonians could get away with something like that!'

Sadly Mick Heaton was killed in a car crash on 10 April 1995. Mick will be remembered for playing an instrumental role in Everton's most successful era and is greatly missed.

Despite some indifferent signings, at the end of his first season in charge, Kendall had taken the club to eighth and the following season he made some of his most astute purchases. Kevin Sheedy moved across Stanley Park for £100,000 and the charismatic Andy King made a return to the Blues.

Future England defender Gary Stevens, who had progressed through the ranks at Everton, established himself in the side, as did fellow graduate, Kevin Ratcliffe, who had switched from left-back to a more comfortable centre half. Ratcliffe's future defensive partner, Derek Mountfield, was signed from Tranmere Rovers for £30,000 while arguably Kendall's best signing, Peter Reid, arrived from Bolton for just £60,000. Everton's new recruits were followed on tour by a couple of young Birds.

Bruges v Everton, pre-season friendly, 1982
Irresistible by Steve Bird

In 1982 I got married down south to a girl from Bristol and ended up buying a house opposite, of all places, Anfield. When pre-season arrived, my mates were off to Bruges to watch Everton play two friendlies and asked me if I was going. My brother Mark, Robert Halligan and Robert Finnigan were off to Belgium so I mentioned I fancied going to my wife of only a few months. She said we couldn't afford it as we had only just got married, so reluctantly I told them I couldn't go. At the time I was working for my old man in a ship repair business on the Dock Road. I got a call in work from the lads to tell me they were off that day and did I fancy meeting them for a drink in a pub in town called The Crocodile during my lunch hour before they set off.

I turned up at The Crocodile dressed in a suit, shirt and tie and met the three lads who were in T-shirts and shorts and clutching Adidas bags ready for the off. One of the lads asked why I wasn't going with them so I explained it was down to money. Being a newlywed with a house, things were a bit tight. With that, he said 'I've just got one of these through the post today,' and reached into his pocket, pulling out a green Access card – 'your flexible friend'. It was one of the first credit cards and I'd never seen one before. 'I'll bung you a few quid on this if you want to go,' he said. 'OK,' I said and with that went home, where I threw on my shorts and a T-shirt before grabbing an overnight bag. Before I left the house I left a note on top of the telly saying 'Gone to Bruges – I just couldn't resist it.'

We had nowhere to stay so spent the first night asleep in a park with a Union Jack flag draped around us. When we woke in the morning I said 'I'm not doing that again. If anyone cops for a girl, they have to sort the rest of the lads out with accommodation.'

We went for a drink and ended up in a bar owned by Raoul Lambert. Lambert had been Bruges' star striker who scored in both legs of the 1976 UEFA Cup final against Liverpool, although sadly these weren't enough for Bruges to beat our adversaries. Out of respect for bagging a few goals against the reds we had a few in his bar before heading to the match, which was against FC Bruges.

At the ground we had a few more drinks but when we went to the bar we had an agreement that whoever's round it was, they had to buy four pints each to save having to go to the bar all the time to get served. When it was my turn I ordered the sixteen pints and set off back to the lads. By this time, though, I was bevvied and lost my bearings. Instead of turning left, I turned right and ended up behind the wrong goal and couldn't find the lads. Thinking they'd gone, I drank all sixteen pints by myself and ended up singing on top of the Everton team's dugout from which I was encouraged to climb down by the local police. Needless to say I can't remember too much about the game itself apart from Steve McMahon hitting the bar and us losing.

After the game I managed to find the lads and we returned to Raoul's bar for a few more drinks. During this time we got friendly with one of the barmen who said later, 'Stevie, my friend down the bar would be very pleased to meet you.'

With that I looked down the bar and there was this fitlooking blonde bird. I raised my glass and she raised hers. I thought 'I'm sorted here' and made my way over. 'Ask her has she gorra flat' came a shout from behind as I approached her. I introduced myself to Corina and we got on well. Sure enough she had a flat around the corner so I asked her if we could get our heads down at hers, to which she agreed.

When we arrived back at her place, I stayed in the master bedroom while my mates fell asleep on the couch. She let us stay there till the end of the tour and when it was time to head back to Liverpool I said my goodbyes to a tearful Corina who had obviously fallen in love with me (and why wouldn't she?).

When I arrived back at my house in Anfield I found a note left by my missus on the telly – 'Gone back to Bristol – just couldn't resist it.' I phoned her to ask what was happening. She said 'You pissed off, so I pissed off.'

'OK,' I said, 'that'll do me' and the following day got straight back over to Bruges and knocked on Corina's door. I ended up living with her for six months, and played semi-professional football for a team in Bruges. I wasn't the best of players but they played me at the back as I was the only one that could head a ball and because of this they kind of built a team around me.

During the season we entered into a tournament playing against teams from across Europe including a side from Stoke-on-Trent. During the game I was marking a bald-headed beast of a fella who kept elbowing me, calling me a dirty Belgian so-and-so, but I kept quiet. This carried on for about 20 minutes until I'd had enough and threw him on the deck, saying, 'Touch me again and I'll break your . . .'

'Oh no,' he said, 'not a bloody Scouser!' After that he left me alone.

By the time this match was being played the romance with Corina was well and truly over and I was missing Everton. So after the final whistle I asked these lads where they were staying and when they were leaving for England. They said they were staying in Ostend and travelling back the following day. So, after Corina left for work early the following morning, I packed my bags and headed to Ostend to meet up with the lads from Stoke who took me back to England.

All in all it ended up as a six-month away game although my dad is still waiting for me to return from my lunch hour!

Steve has now settled down and lives in Childwall with his fourth wife.

In the FA Cup, Everton reached the sixth round but were defeated 1-0 at Old Trafford despite the valiant efforts of keeper Jim Arnold, who produced some excellent saves to keep United at bay. In the league, they reached seventh but hadn't won anything since the League Championship success in 1970. While they were improving, high expectations meant that the 1983–84 season could prove to be make-or-break for Kendall.

To kick-start the new campaign, Kendall took the Blues and a large contingent of supporters to an area of Europe that would become familiar territory to Blues in the coming years.

When I was an apprentice at Preston I lived in digs and a mate of mine lived around the corner. One night we decided to watch Everton versus Manchester United at Goodison Park. We knew we could only watch the first half but we came by train to watch for 45 minutes and I remember Alex Young scoring a header. In the ground, the atmosphere was that much, I remember thinking, I'd love to be a part of this some time.

Howard Kendall, interview, August 2008

Pre-season tournament, Dordrecht, 1983
Turning the Airwaves Blue by Mick Upfield

In August 1983, a friendly at Walsall was followed by a two-match trip to Dordrecht, Holland. As in previous years, pre-season matches were accessed by rail and ferry. My memory of the five days away is a bit patchy, which is probably down to enjoying too much Dutch hospitality and a complete lack of sleep.

We travelled from Harwich to the Hook of Holland and arrived early the next morning. It was summer and the drinking from balmy evening through to dawn was taking its toll. My travel companion on this trip was Paul Gavin, aka 'Marty', and we teamed up with John, from Coventry, and Nick Brennan, a stalwart from ESCLA. I had known Marty for about three years or so and he drank with us in Marbella on a previous pre-season trip which Nick had also been on. John I knew by sight and, as is the case when watching Everton, that is enough to be accepted as 'one of us'. He became the fourth member of our tour.

We made our way by train to The Hague and found cheap accommodation in the Turkish sector above a kebab house. It wasn't the Ritz but it was home for a couple of nights. The owner had this annoying habit of greeting you 'Heeeeelllooooooo' in a squeaky voice, but he was sound. Once we were settled, it was time to take in the sights.

Scheveningen is a friendly place and the Dutch are very polite and affable, so it didn't take long to get into conversation with the locals in the bars. The nightclubs also have a weird system of marking a beer-mat type receipt with your drinks, which you pay for as you leave. As resourceful Blues, we didn't pay very much for our drinks courtesy of a receipt we found which was blank.

The following day, we made our way out to the Dordrecht stadium which was about three miles away. On arrival, we sought the nearest bar and sat in the August sunshine taking in the atmosphere. There were a few Evertonians milling around and a few Dutch lads kicking a ball about on a deserted area of grassland. It wasn't long before a football match of about 30-a-side broke out. We sat back and watched, as it was far too warm to take part. Besides, the beer was cold and this was our summer break.

We entered the stadium and were stunned by the numbers of travelling Evertonians. There were about 400 and that was a conservative estimate. Everton has always been a wellsupported team on their travels, which surprises fans from other clubs as we are/were not that successful trophy wise.

The match passed very quickly, probably due to the copious amount of beer consumed during the day. Everton won 3-1, which meant we would face DS Dordrecht in the final.

Next morning we left for a day out in Amsterdam. The train took about an hour to reach the capital and, once there, we wandered around the red light district for a couple of hours to take in the architecture and sample the local brew. Over the next few hours we took in more and more architecture and sampled even more local brew.

In Dordrecht the following day, we quaffed a few more Amstels and made our way to the ground. As we were playing the host club, the interest in the match had grown and there was a sizeable crowd making their way there too. As is the familiar story with these matches, the beer was more memorable than the footy and Everton lost in a penalty shoot-out.

After the match we could hear a hell of a commotion coming from the local train station. There was loud shouting and swearing as police sirens filled the night air. Peering out of the window at the darkened station we could make out silhouettes of Dutch police systematically sweeping through the platforms. They were with us within minutes and frogmarched us out of the station and into a waiting police van.

In the van were about six or seven others and we were taken to a police station about ten minutes away. On arrival, one of the lads noticed a cannabis plant in the car park and, undetected, picked a couple of leaves for later. We were herded into an open-air compound to be greeted by cheers from about thirty others.

I asked one or two of our 'cellmates' what was happening and he informed me that there had been damage to one of the town bars. The police wanted about 1,000 guilders to pay for the damage and we would not be released until payment had been received. I asked if they had been searched or questioned after being brought in but none of them had. We still had cigarettes, lighters and more importantly passports. I was more at ease with the situation with this knowledge, as I didn't think much could happen if people still had their passports. Unfortunately, we hadn't, as our passports were still in Rotterdam.

The compound door opened and an elderly Dutch policeman entered. In perfect English, he explained that if we managed to raise 500 guilders for the damage, we would all be released. An interesting proposal; pay about £120 between 30 or 40 of us and we could go.

'No way,' came a shout from one side of the compound and the rest of us agreed. The door closed.

One of the lads, who was digging through the bins, found a bundle of newspapers. He said that he was cold, gathered a few papers together and in the middle of the floor set them alight. A long thin plume of smoke exited the compound through the open roof to a chorus of 'Ging gang goolly goolly goolly' from about 20 of us sitting around the fire. The door opened again and two younger policemen came bounding in to stamp out the fire. This was greeted by boos and complaints that it was getting cold.

Two minutes later, the door opened again and a flat, leather football was thrown in. Loud cheers went up and a game started. There were no sides, just fortyodd lads kicking lumps out of each other. After about ten minutes of this, people got bored and someone suggested a game of S.P.O.T.

Looking around the compound there was the door (too small), the back wall (too big) . . . the plate glass observation window . . . just right.

Bang . . . bang . . . thump . . . bang . . . 'S' the game was on, watched nervously through the window by Dordrecht's finest. The shots got harder and hammered against the glass and, within three minutes, the door flew open. 'Stop, Stop!! You can all go now.' A large cheer went up and everyone started singing 'Ev-er-ton, Ev-er-ton.'

Out in the car park we soon realised that we didn't have a clue where we were or how to get to the trains. It was about 7 a.m. and we had to get off to Rotterdam pretty smartish to get our gear in time for our midday ferry. I approached one of the policemen who had gathered to supervise our departure and asked for directions to the railway station. He calmly said that he would take us in the police van. Now, I know I have stated that the Dutch were friendly, but to arrest you, lock you up, then offer you a lift back to the train, that was just too much to ask for.

True to his word, about eight of us bundled into the back of the van with two officers with us for company. As we drove out of the car park a crackled message came over the radio. The policeman in the front passenger seat turned to us and said that officers back at the station were requesting a rendition of the Everton song we had sung in the compound. To show there were no hard feelings, a chorus of 'EV-ER-TON, EV-ER-TON, EV-ER-TON' boomed out accompanied by banging the sides of the van. When we arrived at the train station, some of the more sensible ones who had booked hotels could not believe their eyes or ears as the van pulled up. One of them even thought we had stolen it, until he saw the police in there with us.

We shook hands with our new friends in the Dutch police, who could well have taken us on at 100-a-side footy two years later in Rotterdam before the Cup Winners' Cup final. We managed to get our train and ferry and took home some surreal memories of a night out watching the Blues.

Later that season we were to see the start of the most successful period in our history. Now there lies another story.

In the summer of 1983, Everton brought in Trevor Steven, a fast and skilful midfield player for £300,000 from Burnley. The opening months of the following season were difficult times for Everton fans but they were excited by the arrival of cult hero Andy Gray, who scored on his debut in November. Despite the arrival of the brave Scot, only 13,659 fans attended the December goalless draw with Coventry City at Goodison, the majority of them jeering the team off the pitch at the final whistle.

It has been well documented that in the 1983–84 season Howard Kendall's position as manager was in jeopardy. Despite pressure from expectant supporters, chairman Philip Carter and the players stood by Kendall, who was to rejuvenate Everton over the remaining months of the season. For many fans, two games in particular stand out as the catalysts for Everton's remarkable turnaround.

A League Cup tie at Oxford United was certainly one; a late goal forcing a replay. Everton won that to give their season fresh impetus; so much so that the team progressed to seventh in the table and secured two trips to Wembley. That all-important late goal was scored by the diminutive Adrian Heath, getting on the end of a poor Kevin Brock backpass.

It could very easily be argued that Heath was one of the most important figures in the club's history. That goal at Oxford was a key factor in changing the fortunes at Goodison and providing the team with much-needed optimism and momentum.

Adrian Heath was born in Stoke-on-Trent and after beginning his career with his hometown club, Stoke City, was one of Howard Kendall's first recruits as Everton boss. He signed in 1982 for a then club record fee of £700,000. Adrian became a very important and versatile member of the Everton squad during the eighties, eventually winning two League Championships, the European Cup Winners' Cup and the FA Cup.

He left Everton in 1988 to embark on a career in Spain with Espanyol and later moved back to England, playing for clubs such as Aston Villa and making a return to Stoke along the way. He returned to Everton as Howard Kendall's assistant in Kendall's third spell as manager, helping maintain the Blues' top-flight status on the last day of the season in 1998.

Here, 'Inchy' talks us through the lead-up to the Oxford game and two unexpected new signings.

Milk Cup Quarter Final, Oxford United v Everton, 18 January 1984
Oxford Blues by Adrian Heath

The mood on the team coach on the way to the Manor Ground was quite solemn, probably because this was such a big game for Everton. Earlier in the season, when results and performances were below Everton's high standards, fans had called for the resignation of manager Howard Kendall and chairman Philip Carter. Consequently, Howard was under pressure but so were we. Oxford, with their aggressive defence, were on a decent cup run, so we knew we were up against it and, therefore, apprehensive to say the least. Because of the importance of this game to Everton and Oxford, the match was a sell-out.

As the team bus pulled into the car park we could see several Everton supporters milling about. It was as we got off the bus in the car park, with many fans gathering around to offer words of encouragement, that I noticed two well-known scousers, Tommy Griff and Joe Murray, both big Everton supporters. Tommy and Joe were well known to the players as they knew the likes of Howard Kendall, Colin Harvey and Joe Royle and would often come to Bellefield for a cup of tea and to share some stories. Like many fans, they were without tickets but decided to improvise to get in to see the game. When the bus stopped, they lifted up the storage compartments under the coach and took out the skips which held the team's kit and players' boots. Impersonating members of Everton staff they took hold of them and, calm as you like, walked straight into the Manor Ground without anyone questioning what they were doing. I and a few of the other players just laughed and made our own way into the dressing rooms to prepare for the game. Tommy and Joe, who could get into places water couldn't, left quickly and we presumed they had just mingled in with the other Everton fans on the terraces.

Before kick-off, the Everton squad went out on to the field to complete the pre-match warm-up routine. As I was doing some stretches I glanced up and there they were, bold as brass, Tommy and Joe. They were stood on the pitch talking to each other, pressing their heels into the turf whilst nodding in agreement as if to say, 'Yeah, that's all right that.' Obviously not content with just free entry into the game, I later looked over and there they were again, this time having their photos taken on the pitch with Howard Kendall, Oxford's manager Jim Smith and the Oxford chairman Robert Maxwell. I just laughed at their confidence and new-found status as honorary directors of Everton as they paraded in front of the fans before taking their seats in the directors' box to watch the game.

Other less adventurous Evertonians were packed behind the goal to the left of this tight, compact ground. We were well aware that we were well supported that night and that the TV cameras were in attendance too as they were anticipating a possible cup upset. Fortunately this never happened and the result that night gave the team and the fans a real sense of belief.

Earlier that month, Everton had played Stoke City in the third round of the FA Cup in a game that was just as significant as that at Oxford; a game in which the atmosphere created by the Everton fans was an inspiration to the players who were determined to turn their season around. Howard Kendall recalls the events of that fateful game.

Stoke City v Everton, 6 January 1984
Stoke the Fire by Howard Kendall

We were having a rough time of it at that part of the season and the game had taken on huge importance. The players and I were under a lot of pressure.

I've heard that there was a following of almost 10,000 Evertonians and you could just hear them. The dressing room was on the side where the Evertonians were sat, just down the corridor, and you could already hear them singing and shouting. So I just thought to myself, 'How important is it to you lads sitting in this dressing room? Is it as important to you as it is to that lot out there?'

I thought 'Right, let them hear how important it is.' I just opened the window and let them hear the roar.

I didn't think it was a big issue at the time but the players all talked about it afterwards. They even said it was the best team talk I had ever done! I prepared all the players the day before and I did have a team talk in mind that day. It consisted of me reminding them of their roles and responsibilities a few minutes before we went out on to the field but I just decided to let the fans do the talking. It was just off the cuff really, it wasn't planned.

I think the knowledge that they had so much support behind them ensured that the players relaxed a little and it eased a bit of tension before an important game. They knew that the Evertonians would be behind them even if things weren't going right. I just think that if you can't be inspired by that then you shouldn't be on the field.

The feeling at the end of the game was obviously joy at winning but also, for me personally, a sense of relief. The media fancied an upset in this game – but they were disappointed and we were in the next round of the Cup.

Howard Kendall's achievements as Everton manager are unparalleled, without question. Not only was Howard the only manager to sleep with the FA Cup the night it was won, but his special relationship with Blues fans quickly made Evertonians take him to their hearts. This was exemplified when he took over the captaincy from Everton legend Brian Labone.

When I took over the armband from Labby, he just said one thing to me. 'Make sure Eddie Cavanagh gets a ticket – home or away!' I've done it for years and I want you to carry that on.' So I did.

Further examples of Howard's special bond with Evertonians include the occasion the team attended the PFA awards in London in 1985. Sat at the 'Everton' table was Tommy Griff, a regular fan who was very popular with players and staff alike. Here, Howard tells the story of that night at the prestigious end-of-season awards ceremony.

Tommy was a great character and unbelievably devoted to Everton. He lived and breathed the club and still does. So we were at the PFA awards and we remembered, having been there the previous year, that it was nigh on impossible to get served alcohol after a certain time. At 12 p.m. the bar closed and as it was a Sunday night there was nowhere open. A friend of mine from Birmingham suggested we put in a big order at the bar and stash the beers and miniatures under the table so that we didn't need to bother them again.

At the end of the night we were the only table with any drinks left; to the point where our table was three deep with people wanting drinks. Two of those were the then England manager Bobby Robson and his assistant Don Howe. So Tommy went over to Bobby Robson, made sure the England manager was fixed with a drink and pulling up the sleeve on his left arm said, 'D'ya wanna buy a watch, Bobby lad? I've got loads of snide Cartiers and that, you know.' Totally baffled, Bobby replied that he'd just bought a watch. Unperturbed, Tommy, pulling up his right sleeve said, 'What about one for your missus!'

Now, the beauty of Tommy was that he was totally genuine and serious and didn't ever realise he was being funny.

'Are you comin' up for the Derby then, Bobby?'

'Err, yes I may do.'

'Well, I tell you what. If you come up for the game and get stuck for a brief (ticket), let me know and I'll sort yer out. Now, here's my number and keep this to yourself, all right? Are you comin' up with yer tart, yer know, yer Missus? If you are, you're more than welcome to stay with us!'

We were falling about laughing but Tommy was deadly serious. There's the England manager being offered the chance to stay in a council house in Norris Green! Absolutely hilarious it was.

Howard also recounts a short story about Tommy Griff's close friend and Everton fanatic, Joe Murray.

One afternoon, I was in my office in Bellefield and all I could hear was this laughter during lunchtime after the lads had finished training – and I just knew that Joey was there. Now, at this time, we had Graeme Sharp and Andy Gray playing up front for us. We had a pool table and both Graeme and Andy were different class at it. They would boast about being the champions and threaten to take on anyone. So Joey piped up that day, 'Me and my mate will beat you two.'

So the two lads agree and decide to stake a tenner on it. The next day comes and Joey walks in – with John Parrott! I've never seen Andy and Graeme so lost for words. Needless to say John Parrott cleaned up and Joey won his bet.

It's unbelievable. I tend to bump into a lot of football fans and the nice thing is that I get remembered more for playing for Everton, than I do for Arsenal. It's such a welcoming club that I'll never forget it. It's a special place. I captained the club and that was another fantastic milestone. To be the first black captain is something that I will cherish forever and it was a privilege every time I was able to pull the armband on.

Kevin Campbell, Liverpool Echo, January 2009

In the semi-final, Everton faced Aston Villa, the team that had broken their hearts in the same competition seven years earlier. The prospect of another Wembley final was something for both the players and fans to sing about.

Aston Villa v Everton, 22 February 1984
Football League 'Milk' Cup Semi-Final 2nd Leg
Reidy sings the Blues by Kenny Evans

Having secured a 2-0 lead from the first leg thanks to an excellent 'save' by Kevin Richardson, we embarked on a trip to Villa Park on a Wednesday night. My Sunday league footy manager at the time had wangled me an invite to a corporate box at Villa, who at the time were one of the few clubs to have such a facility. I duly put on my best bib and tucker and proceeded to drive to Villa Park. How was I to know at these functions they ply you with beer like it is going out of fashion? I'd parked up several streets away from Villa Park as my hosts didn't supply me with a parking permit – the bastards. It turned out our hosts for the night were not even Villa fans but Birmingham City fans. Imagine that.

Our 'box' consisted of a few Villa fans but mainly us Blues who had been invited courtesy of this firm. Below us and above us were thousands of us, all anticipating that we could get to Wembley for the first time in seven years; the noise was incredible. All the gadgets and gizmos were new to us – crowd control volume, live TV, air con and a girl that served beer at your seat – whey hey! What more could we want? A Wembley appearance would do nicely.

History will deem that we did reach that final. At the final whistle, I jumped up, arms outstretched, only to punch the polystyrene ceiling tile . . . oops. Sorry there Mister Brum, not only have you plied me with beer, fed me, entertained me and I wreck your private box. I wonder why I never got invited back?

Below me were thousand of Blues going mad and all I wanted to do was join them. Alas, I had to show some restraint and go along with my hosts and chat about some trivial subjects. Small talk is not my forte and when the conversation touched on Crufts, I made my apologies, thanked my hosts and made my way into the night. The ground had emptied by now, except for a few stragglers. As I made my way across the car park, there was the Everton coach and Reidy was just about to board.

'Peter, you were fuckin' great tonight!' to which he replied, whilst grabbing me by the shoulders, 'No, you were . . . every fuckin' one of yer! Every Evertonian here tonight played a blinder!'

We just stood there hugging and kissing . . .

'Can you do us a favour, Pete, and get my programme signed?' I asked, pointing to the players on the coach.

'Get on yerself.'

So I did.

The champers was already flowing as Reidy started the singing. Behind me, I felt someone board the coach as it rocked when someone gets on.

'I hope we are gonna stop off for some fuckin' chips tonight!'

It was Big Nev, and only he could have come out with that.

Being starstruck and inebriated, I had forgotten where I had parked my car . . . doh! Roaming round Aston ain't my idea of partying. Twenty or so minutes later, I found it. Now I could party.

Singing all the way home, it was a joy to drive. Even if I had been breathalised I'd have been happy to provide the ossifer with a sample of pure joy.

The bar was kept open on my arrival back home and how we sang! Nights like these make you an Evertonian – it's ingrained in all of us.

In the League Cup final, the first of their two Wembley visits in 1984, Everton met their Merseyside rivals, Liverpool. It was the first all-Merseyside match under the Twin Towers and the beginning of a battle for supremacy during this fine era for both teams. After the first game ended goalless, the Toffees were unfortunate to lose 1-0 in the replay.

However, the Blues made amends in their second Wembley appearance that year. Everton's first FA Cup final for 16 years saw them face Elton John's Watford, managed by a young Graham Taylor. A Graeme Sharp goal in the first half and a slightly controversial Andy Gray header were enough to lift the Cup for the Blues. The win proved to be the catalyst for the most successful era in their rich history. Here, two loyal fans, who attended both finals, reminisce about a momentous period in the Club's history and reveal the story behind one of Everton's most famous images.

Liverpool is the same kind of support but Everton is a bit more aggressive because Everton is up at the moment. Over the last one or two years, especially, it has been one of the noisiest grounds and has a great atmosphere. Liverpool is the same but now a little bit more genteel.

Arsène Wenger, January 2008

Milk Cup Final, Liverpool v Everton, 25 March 1984
Lodgers by Graham Moore

It was March 1984 and every Blue and Red I knew was doing the same thing, travelling to London for the first ever all-Merseyside Wembley final. Lime Street was awash with noise and colour as thousands of Blues and Reds travelled down together.

Most fans I knew were going without a ticket or anywhere to stay – those details just weren't important. Nobody wanted to miss out. We listened to a hand-held radio while waiting for the train to depart – the landmark jingle '1 9 4, Radio City' came on with the headlines, 'The streets of Liverpool are deserted this morning as thousands of Merseyside football fans invade the Capital . . .'

We all knew it was a special occasion, and, Red or Blue, it felt magic being part of it. There was an extra swagger as we clambered off at Euston with Londoners stood by in amazement as two armies joined forces to raise the roof of the station. Even the police stood and watched in admiration of the camaraderie.

There were about fifteen lads in our crew – all from Birkenhead's notorious Woodchurch Estate. I can remember travelling down dressed in a Fred Perry T-shirt, Lois jeans and Adidas Samba. Thankfully we had a game plan; we would book a room before the rush, as soon as we got off the train. Dixie (Davie Hawthorne) and I headed for the hotel district in King's Cross and searched for those with vacancies. After about ten goes we realised that as soon as the hoteliers heard our accent they turned us away.

Just as we were about to give up – a flash of inspiration. We saw an advert for the British Badminton Championships. From then on we changed our accents and I became the brother of British Badminton's golden girl, Gillian Gilks – down to watch 'my sister' compete in the championships. It worked first time as this woman allowed us to put a mattress in her basement dining room. She made us promise that we wouldn't eat any of the food until breakfast – and that it would only be the two of us.

After drinking the pubs of Soho and Covent Garden dry, fifteen of us piled into that basement and ate everything we could get our hands on! At about 7.30 a.m. the others scarpered, leaving just a trail of crumbs behind them, but Dixie and I had the cheek to stay and have breakfast. Well, why not – we had paid for it!

Everton v Watford, FA Cup Final, 19 May 1984
Raise your Glasses by Steve Judge

I travelled by coach with our Alan and the usual lads who followed Everton away. It was great to see the Blues back at Wembley again in such a short space of time and we were hoping for better fortune this time around. I had been to the Milk Cup final replay defeat at Maine Road and witnessed the 0-0 draw in the League Cup final at Wembley against Aston Villa in 1977. However, this time we felt particularly confident and optimistic as, in my opinion, we had done all the hard work and losing to Watford would be sickening, no disrespect to them.

When we arrived in the capital we had a few drinks in the pubs close to the stadium before making our way to Wembley. There was a great atmosphere outside the ground with friendly banter being exchanged between both sets of supporters, described as two of the friendliest in the country.

One or two of the lads who went to Wembley did so without tickets so we walked around the stadium in search of spares. As we walked in front of the twin towers we saw several showbiz celebrities making their way into the ground, one of whom was Warren Mitchell who played Alf Garnett in the sitcom Till Death Us Do Part. He was surrounded by supporters and entering into the banter in good spirits. To be fair to him, he acted just like his character, going on about West Ham and taking any stick in his stride.

When everyone had tickets, we made our way into the stadium and took our positions to the left of the goal opposite the tunnel end. The thousands of Blues there that day ensured the atmosphere was bouncing and you got the feeling it was going to be our day. There were loads of great messages on flags being waved including one that read 'Elton, I guess that's why they call us the Blues' in reference to Elton John, Watford's chairman at the time.

The time at a cup final goes so quickly and before you know it the game is under way. Watford had a couple of chances before Graeme Sharp slotted home in front of the Everton faithful. Our end of the ground erupted as the ball entered the net and the half ended 1-0. By half-time our Alan was in high spirits because of the goal – and all the ale he had put away. He was really enjoying himself and had dressed for the occasion by wearing a pair of enormous comedy sunglasses he had bought from a girl who was wearing them while selling hot dogs at the semi-final victory over Southampton at Highbury.

Watford had had one or two moments themselves in the first half and, with the likes of John Barnes and Mo Johnston in the team, could cause problems for any side. It was therefore a huge relief when Andy Gray scored early in the second half to virtually make the game safe. The atmosphere at this point was electric and remained so until the final whistle when Kevin Ratcliffe lifted Everton's first FA Cup since the famous victory of '66 – their first trophy since the title-winning season of 1970.

Most fans stayed to applaud the team on their lap of honour and as the players celebrated directly in front of us; our Alan bulldozed his way through the crowds to the main barrier. When the players eventually passed our position, he made his way back but without his extra large sunglasses. When I asked him where they were, he told me he had given them to John Bailey who was also wearing a large Everton top hat.

The victory that day helped erase the bitter disappointments of our League Cup defeats in '77 and '84 and we celebrated down Walton Road on our return to the city.

It wasn't until the following day when we saw the Sunday newspapers that the significance of our Alan giving his sunglasses to John Bailey finally hit home. Images of John Bailey wearing the top hat and large glasses like an Elton John lookalike were all over the papers, an image that all Evertonians can instantly recall with great fondness. It even made the front page of the Sunday Mirror which described it as 'a day when the outsized "bins" of Blues full-back John Bailey put Elton John's sunglasses in the shade.'

I kept the newspapers as a lasting souvenir of that great day nearly a quarter of a century ago. Hopefully, it won't be too long before we're enjoying another happy day in May.

The sight of John Bailey in his oversized glasses and his comedy top hat has gone down in Everton folklore as a lasting image which encompassed the joy felt by all Evertonians on their Wembley success. Here, Everton's 'Joker in the Pack' recalls his personal memories.

Freddie the Starr by John Bailey

I was released by Everton as a 15-year-old and, after a brief spell playing Sunday football in Liverpool, signed apprenticeship forms with Blackburn Rovers. After completing my apprenticeship, I returned to Everton in 1979. Blackburn wanted £500,000 for me, but Everton weren't prepared to pay that, so the transfer went to a tribunal which concluded that Everton had to pay an initial £200,000, with a further £100,000 to be paid after I had played 50 games.

When I returned to Bellefield I was in awe of the place and its players. Sitting in the changing rooms next to the likes of Bob Latchford, Martin Dobson and Colin Todd, who were all England internationals, was a nervous experience. However, they were great lads and made me feel welcome straight away.

It wasn't long before I established myself in the team and chalked up the 50 games which triggered the extra £100,000 payment to Blackburn.

Howard Kendall replaced Gordon Lee as manager and he started to bring in some great players who were also great lads. The camaraderie of the players was great. All the squad would go out for a few drinks midweek if there was no game. Even the likes of Neville Southall, who was teetotal, would join us just to socialise with the lads. I think this togetherness off the field helped us on the field too.

We were narrowly beaten in the Milk Cup final replay to Liverpool so were determined to win the FA Cup in May.

The night before a game, I would take a tablet to help me relax and sleep, but the night before the FA Cup final, I didn't, because the boss allowed us to have a drink. When we were having our evening meal Howard said 'You can have one drink and that's it. And that means you too Bailsy!'

Luckily Graeme Sharp didn't want his and slid his pint down to me so I had two.

Thanks to the couple of lagers I slept well but we were woken around 8 a.m. by laughter outside our hotel. I was sharing a room with Andy Gray and we went to our window to see what was going on. When we opened the window we noticed the other players hanging out of their rooms laughing at what was going on down below. Normally I was the one renowned for cracking jokes, but the players didn't have to rely on me to keep them entertained that day as we'd been sent our own comedian, Evertonian Freddie Starr – our opponents Watford had been sent Michael Barrymore. Freddie was on the grass running around dressed as a football player from the 1900s. When he looked up to our room he noticed Andy Gray's distinctive blond hair and shouted 'You think you look like me!'

Later that morning, after we had changed, we were asked to go downstairs. When we arrived, Freddie was dressed as a manager from the 1900s in a suit with a bowler hat on and a gold pocket watch. He delivered a team talk to the players and we couldn't stop laughing at his antics.

When we drove to Wembley, Freddie wasn't on our bus but he turned up again in the changing rooms before the kick-off. He was heading the ball and even came out on to the pitch with us. If he could have put a shirt on that day and played for us I'm sure he would have. Freddie played a big part that day as he took a lot of the pressure off the players.

Walking out at Wembley that day in front of all those Evertonians was an unbelievable feeling but the whole thing goes so fast it's over before you know it.

After picking up my winners' medal, which I dropped on the floor after kissing it, I made my way down the steps. As players were making their way down the stairs, fans threw scarves and hats for them to wear.

I was given a large top hat, which I put on, followed by a pair of large sunglasses which were thrown at me.

After celebrating on the pitch in front of the fans, I handed the hat to a steward to mind for me while I was interviewed by Bob Wilson on BBC1. After the interview, there was no sign of the steward or the hat although some time afterwards I received a letter from someone saying he had it but wasn't going to return it. The fella who had made the hat in a cardboard factory where he worked also got in touch with me with a photo of himself wearing it before the final. Many fans have since asked me about the hat but I don't know where it is. Perhaps it will turn up on eBay one day.

I couldn't wait to return home for the celebrations and get into the city centre where I knew my family would be waiting. The scenes that day were fantastic as thousands of fans came out to celebrate Everton's long-overdue success. Some fans were like monkeys, climbing up on to all kinds of things to get a good view of the team and the FA Cup. As we passed pubs, fans threw cans and bottles of lager up to the players and I was like the Pope, blessing the Blue congregation. It took about a week for me get a proper night's sleep as I was high on emotion with the adrenalin still pumping.

I left Everton with FA Cup and League Championship winners' medals and, although I continued my career elsewhere, it was never the same as being with Everton.

I still follow Everton and go to every home game hoping the current squad will eventually enjoy some of the success we did.

On Yer Bike by Graham Moore

Having lost out to Liverpool in the Milk Cup final it was almost a dream to have another bite of the cherry in the same season. Like a number 10 bus, we waited for years to go to Wembley then we got two chances in one season! On the way to Highbury to watch the Blues against Southampton, none of us really believed we would do it. Dixie

(Dave Hawthorne) and I boasted that if we won we would cycle to Wembley.

When Adrian Heath popped up in extra time to head into the North Bank we went crazy and minutes later after the whistle, we invaded the pitch. I lost Dixie in the madness and it was only when I got back into the North Bank that I met him again – both of us were going wild and it was in that moment we committed to make the journey to Wembley on our bikes.

We had only about four weeks to train for it – and Dixie didn't even have a bike! He was a legend, though, and mainly down to him we raised over a thousand pounds for the special baby care unit at Arrowe Park Hospital. He also got us covered in the Echo and on Radio Merseyside – where a young Ray Stubbs worked. He came and interviewed us during a training session.

We even went to Bellefield and met many of our heroes – Andy King was there but had just found out that he wouldn't be playing in the final so he wasn't too happy to talk to us – but others like John Bailey and Andy Gray were more than happy to be sponsors.

We set off on the Wednesday before the game and got to Birmingham in one day, kipping at my auntie's. The next day was much tougher with massive hills and the pair of us were knackered. We eventually got to St Albans where we had a fight with each other because I fell asleep by the side of the road while Dixie was trying to sort out some digs.

The next day, all our mates were waiting for us on Wembley Way as we cycled down the day before the match. It was an amazing feeling to know we had achieved the dream. We all then headed to our favourite boozer in King's Cross – we were treated like heroes by all the lads in the pub – we even got our photo taken with Phil Daniels, the cult hero from Quadrophenia who later went on to play Kevin Wicks in EastEnders.

On the Saturday, we cycled to the ground and were recognised by hundreds of Evertonians on Wembley Way. We cycled up to the main entrance and asked former Everton captain Mark Higgins if he could hide our bikes somewhere – he took them in and we got them after the game.

After celebrating into the small hours in an Irish pub in Kilburn, we kipped on the floor at Euston. The next morning we were woken by lads shouting, 'Here's the team!' We rushed with our bikes down on to the platform where Andy Gray and John Bailey recognised us and brought out the FA Cup for us to hold in front of thousands of Evertonians.

We had to bunk on to that train on the way home because we never had a train ticket and when we got home we followed the cavalcade around the city on our bikes. Ray Stubbs was on the team bus and he recognised us too and mentioned us in his live commentary.

A weekend to savour for ever. Never to be forgotten memories. A dream come true for two young Blues!

I include myself and many of my former teammates as fans. I have spoken to many of them since the weekend and they, like me, are delighted. There is something special about Everton. People say 'Once an Evertonian, Always an Evertonian' and it's so true. Everton touches you in a way that no other club could.

Alex Young, Evertonfc.com, May 2005

The following season, Everton embarked upon what was to become the most successful season in the club's history. Domestically, the Blues sealed the League Championship with three games to spare, finishing a full 13 points ahead of Liverpool. It was, however, Everton's European exploits which ensured it was a season not to forget.

Capping off a wonderful summer in the knowledge that the team were Cup winners, Everton played their first European game in Ireland. John Saunders, known by many as the 'Irish Des Lynam', was present to watch the Cup-winning Blues.

European Cup Winners' Cup, 1st Round, 1st leg
UCD v Everton, 19 September 1984
University Challenged by John Saunders

I'm a mad Evertonian. If we're out in public and I see someone wearing an Everton shirt my wife always gets embarrassed. She knows what's going to happen. I just can't resist it. I have to speak to them, hug them even. For example, I was at the World Cup finals at USA '94 with work and after one match I saw a man leaving the stadium wearing an Everton shirt. My wife begged me, but I was off – I wanted to hug him, buy him a drink and chat about Everton.

I work as a broadcaster for RTE over in Ireland and during the 1984–85 season University College Dublin were playing Everton in the first round of the Cup Winners' Cup. A few weeks previously there had been some trouble when Glasgow Rangers had been over to play Bohemians. The police were involved and had to deal with a riot. So, naturally, the UCD and the police were keen to avoid a repeat performance with the hundreds of Evertonians. Leaflets were handed out saying 'UCD welcomes the Gwladys Street' and messages were given over the public address system in an attempt to curb any ill feeling or violence.

I was chatting to the UCD manager Tony O'Neill a while later and asked if there was any trouble or incident before or after the game. He informed me that there had been one arrest. Apparently one fan's view was blocked by a policeman and the fan told him to 'Get out of the fuckin' way.' The fan was obviously escorted out of the ground. However, the funny thing was it wasn't an Evertonian who'd been arrested but a lecturer from the University College!

I remember thinking once what it meant to be an Evertonian. I realised at the FA Cup final in 1995. I was given excellent tickets by the club and was sat directly behind the goal with my son who was about 14 at the time. He now lives and works in Beijing. When the final whistle went my son burst into tears. This was unusual for him and I thought it was such an unbelievable show of emotion from such a little guy. When quizzed why he was crying he said that he was sick of having the piss taken out of him in school for being an Evertonian. All his friends at school supported Liverpool or Man Utd and it was a build-up of years of torment in that very emotional moment. He loves the Blues as much as I do.

In the 2007–08 season we drew West Ham in the Carling Cup and actually played them twice in a week at Upton Park. Through my work I have many contacts throughout Europe and one is based in our Warsaw office in Poland. His name is Wojcik and he is a big Everton fan. I discovered that Wojcik was over in London for a conference the day of the game and was keen to surprise him. He had never been to an Everton game before but had been a fan for years. He was very excited being over in London for the first time but I wanted to make it extra special for him. I rang his boss and informed him that Wojcik had another important meeting to go to and would be unable to attend the conference. I then spoke to Wojcik and told him I was taking him out and he needed to bring a tie.

We arrived at Upton Park and his face lit up. I was a guest of West Ham for the game and had seats in the directors' box. Wojcik had a fantastic time. From never having been to a game before, there he was sat in the directors' box next to Bill Kenwright watching the Blues defeat West Ham for the second time in a week. I asked Wojcik once how he became an Everton fan. He said that years ago he wrote off to every Premiership Club asking for more details on the club. Everton were the only team to respond.

After an excellent win against a very strong Bayern Munich side in the semi-final of the Cup Winners' Cup, the Blues travelled to Rotterdam and faced Rapid Vienna. A truly memorable night ended in a 3-1 win for the Blues thanks to goals from Andy Gray, Trevor Steven and one from Kevin Sheedy's trusty left foot. The team of '85 were on for an unprecedented treble which looked a probability when Manchester United were reduced to ten men in the FA Cup final. However, they were denied courtesy of a special goal by teenager Norman Whiteside. Nonetheless, it was the European tour which captured the imagination of the Blues supporters, players and staff alike, that culminated in a magical night in Rotterdam.

European Cup Winners' Cup Final, Rapid Vienna v Everton, 15 May 1985
Bridgey by Graham Smith

I always remember amusing incidents because I have that sort of sense of humour and this story is certainly amusing. It shows the lengths Evertonians will go to in order to watch the Blues.

Now Howard Kendall was really big on continuity throughout the football club – be it set pieces or drills – it was the same for the first team right down to the youth players. So when we had end-of-season trips to places such as Magaluf all the members of the club were involved. It was the same if we made it to a cup final. I was youth team coach but was invited when the first team made it to Wembley, and wives and girlfriends were invited too. This created an excellent camaraderie in that respect which all the players and staff appreciated. In any case, Howard and Colin always made sure you were well looked after.

So I was asked to sit on the bench for cup finals and also be in the dressing room. I felt a real part of the whole first team scene. This was so that I could hear all that was being said, which was always useful. Howard always encouraged this continuity because I was producing youth team players who would subsequently play for the reserves and eventually the first team.

We were away in Rotterdam for the Cup Winners' Cup final against Rapid Vienna in 1985. Vienna had a player called Hans Krankl playing for them who was earmarked as their danger man. I was sat in the dressing room corner listening in to the team talk, taking mental notes, while the discussion moved on to negating the threat posed

Looking Sharp. Bob Latchford with a very young Graeme Sharp
on tour in Marbella..

(top) Everton legends. Alan Ball pictured with legendary Everton fan Eddie Cavanagh. Bally was Godfather to Eddie's child.
(bottom) We made it at last! Graham Moore celebrating in London with former Eastenders actor, Phil Daniels.

(top) Where's the bar? An inquisitive Steve Bird standing on the tunnel behind the Everton team's dugout before the friendly against Bruges and drinking 16 pints! (bottom) "The Toffee Suite". Ray Parr posing in his mini-Everton museum near Goodison Park called "The Striker's Suite". The chair previously resided in the office of an ex-Everton chairman.

¡ Fl Liverpool es mierda! Even the Spanish know their history.

Liverpool Football Club
and Athletic Grounds Co. Ltd

Manager : W. Shankly
Secretary : P. B. Robinson
Telephone : 051-263 2361/2

ANFIELD ROAD
LIVERPOOL L4 0TH

16-3-70.

Dear Oliver,

       Find enclosed one ticket as requested, at least you are honest in your request.

Yours truly,

B Shankly
Manager

(top) Perhaps they're not all bad. A letter and ticket for the Derby from former Liverpool manager, Bill Shankly.
(bottom) Pictured outside the Winslow Hotel before a match is Gerry Foran (left), Michael Koeslag and a young Wayne Rooney

(top) Midfield maestros and Everton legends. Peter Reid and Howard Kendall pictured in The Striker's Suite before the FA Cup quarter-final against Middlesbrough, 2009.

(bottom) "On my swede!" Members of the Swedish Toffees meet with one of our Swedish idols – '95 Cup winner Anders Limpar.

(top) Alec Cairns with some Metalist Kharkiv fans in the main square in Kharkiv, Ukraine before his friend Alan Midgley performed a disappearing act.
(bottom) ¡Vamos los Blues! Gordon Lee takes in some Spanish culture on tour with Everton in Marbella.

(top) Gerry Foran and his partner Pam in Greece with Howard Kendall when Howard was manager of Greek side Xanthi.
(bottom) The Everton Boys are in town! Tom Sellick proudly waving the Everton flag before the UEFA Cup match against Standard Liege.

by Krankl. It was the same scenario on the bench. The atmosphere was fantastic while the players went out to warm up and everyone was soaking it up.

Colin always liked to sit near the halfway line and obviously Howard would be with him and I was sat at the opposite end of the bench. Just before the game kicked off I looked to my right and wondered who the fella was sat next to me who I'd never seen before. Then he winked at me. As he was dressed in full white and grey Everton Le Coq Sportif tracksuit I just said hello and got on with watching the game. Obviously because of the enormity of the game I couldn't stop and ask Colin or Howard, 'Who is this character?'

The game went on and, as all Evertonians know, we won 3-1 and this fella is doing cartwheels each time we score.

After the game I asked Colin, 'That fella in the tracksuit on the end, who is he?' Colin replied, as a matter of fact, 'Oh that's Bridgey.' Now Bridgey was just a fan, a chancer. He was a bit like the Man Utd fan who posed for the cameras in full Man Utd kit alongside Gary Neville a few years back, pretending to be part of the squad.

Yet Bridgey pre-dated this fella by 15 years. You always hear tales of Scouse fans in Cup finals carrying a bag of balls and saying the words, 'Match balls, mate' if anyone asks but Bridgey actually did it, nonchalantly sat there with the best seat in the house. Whether he had a ticket or bunked in or just wanted to do it for bravado I'm not sure but it was certainly something to tell the grandchildren.

I was over there for the Cup Winners' Cup final in Rotterdam in 1985. At four in the morning we were waiting for the plane home but no one cared if the plane came or not because we'd won.

Brian Labone, Evertonfc.com, May 2005

Everton's return to Europe's premier competition was halted by a European ban on all English clubs as a consequence of the Heysel disaster. Liverpool and Juventus faced each other in the European Cup final and shortly before kick-off a fence separating the two sets of supporters was breached by Liverpool's fans. Italian fans were forced to retreat and the result was that a supporting wall collapsed killing 39 supporters. A very sad day.

Despite the circumstances, in the close season Everton still managed to persuade England's hottest property, Gary Lineker, to sign. Lineker put pen to paper in a deal worth £800,000 for his boyhood club, Leicester City, while Everton's hero from the previous season, Andy Gray, moved on to Aston Villa. In Lineker's only season with the Blues he was a goal machine. He scored 40 times in 52 games in all competitions, including 30 in the league. In the process he became the country's leading marksman as well as the first Everton player since Bob Latchford to reach the magical 30 goals in a season.

Despite Lineker's goal prowess, Everton narrowly missed out on the League championship, finishing runners-up to Kenny Dalglish's Liverpool. It was to get even worse for the blue half of Merseyside as they also lost 3-1 in the FA Cup final to their arch-rivals. The final was to prove to be Lineker's last game in the famous blue shirt as he moved on to the Catalan giants Barcelona in a £2.6m deal.

Watching that Merseyside final was a former Everton player whose own generosity saw him stuck with a typical gloating Liverpudlian.

FA Cup Final v Liverpool, 10 May 1986
Dr No Fun by Mike Lyons

In 1986 I was manager of Second Division Grimsby Town and had been invited to Wembley for the final to provide match commentary for BBC Radio Merseyside. After the game, naturally disappointed, I left Wembley along with John Cooney – a Liverpool fan – and Terry Darracott's brother Laurence, a Blue.

As we were making our way over to my car, Laurence spotted a fella from by where he lived who he sometimes used to drink with. 'He lives by ours,' he said. 'Can we give him a lift?'

I agreed and so Laurence called the guy over to where we were parked. When he arrived I couldn't believe it. He looked like a circus ringmaster dressed in red shoes and trousers wearing a big red top hat. He was also wearing a full-length red coat with tails that was full of badges, on the back of which he had written 'Hiya kids, Liverpool's own Doctor Fun'.

As he approached the car he was clutching a carrier bag containing cans of ale. He got in the car, sat in the back and produced two red and white glove puppets on his hands. Putting on a squeaky voice, he pointed the puppets at me and in the style of a ventriloquist said 'Ah thanks very much. Mick Lyons as well, an Evertonian giving me a lift home, ah that's great that,' moving his hands as he spoke.

I told him it was no problem and off we set. He said he was going to the Oak Tree pub, Huyton, so I said we could drop him off there. We were driving along the motorway and as it was a hot day he asked could he have one of his cans of lager, to which I replied 'Yeah, no problem.'

He must have been shaking them during the match because when he opened one, the lager sprayed out, drenching me and the car. As if that wasn't bad enough, as we passed coaches carrying football fans, he wound down the window, popped his head out and started shouting to the passengers, 'Mick Lyons is giving me a lift home, 3-1!, 3-1!' making the journey home from Wembley the longest and worst imaginable.

By the time we reached Knutsford services I swapped driving with John Cooney, who drove on to Huyton. When we reached the Oak Tree pub, Dr Fun thanked us for the lift and asked if we fancied joining him for a drink. Eager to get away, we declined his invitation so he closed the door behind him and we set off in hurry. A bit worse for wear, Dr Fun didn't realise he had trapped the long tails of his coat in the door and as we sped off down the road he came with us, shouting,

'Mick, Mick, Stop! Stop!'

After realising he was trapped by his coat, we stopped in order for him to release his coat from the door. When Laurence opened the door to set him free, his coat, which was his pride and joy, was ripped right up to the neck leaving him, for once, speechless.

A third of the Lineker money was to be spent on a young centre back from Norwich City by the name of Dave Watson and other new signings included Ian Snodin and Birmingham City's Wayne Clarke; the latter managing to score five important goals in five games in the run-in to the end of the season.

The dominance of the Merseyside clubs continued into the 1986–87 season. Injuries to the likes of Sharp, Sheedy and Stevens couldn't deny the Blues some revenge for the previous season's heartbreak and the league was won in convincing style. In the FA Cup the Blues were defeated by 'The Crazy Gang' of Wimbledon who would put a smile back on Evertonians' faces the next year with a 1-0 over Liverpool in the FA Cup final.

It came as a complete shock not only to Evertonians but to the world of football when Howard Kendall announced he would be leaving the club at the end of the 1986–87 season. He decided to try his hand in the Spanish League with the Basque club Athletic Bilbao and left Colin Harvey to take over the reigns at Goodison.

Colin Harvey was making the step up from assistant to manager but despite an inconsistent start to the season and a disappointing final four games the Blues still managed to finish a respectable fourth in the league. However, a sustained challenge was out of reach as injuries took their toll; especially to integral members of the squad such as Heath, Sheedy and Bracewell.

The 1987–88 and 1988–89 seasons were periods of transition for the club. Among the players to leave during this time were a good few members of the '85 squad including Derek Mountfield, Trevor Steven, Gary Stevens and Peter Reid. However, Harvey had money to spend and was keen to invest wisely; bringing in, among others, the highly rated Tony Cottee from West Ham in a record £2.3m deal, Stuart McCall and Pat Nevin.

The disappointment of an eighth-placed finish in the League was easier to swallow as Everton were once again at Wembley for the 1989 Cup final against Liverpool. The occasion was very much an emotional affair with a sombre atmosphere engendered by the terrible events at Hillsborough a few weeks beforehand. The match itself was in doubt at one stage but eventually went ahead. Everton had played Norwich City in the other semi-final, unaware of the tragedy unfolding at Hillsborough. One young Evertonian and his friend very nearly didn't make it to Villa Park.

FA Cup Semi-Final, Norwich City v Everton, Villa Park, 15 April 1989
The Yob by David Cregeen

On the morning of the semi-final I boarded a coach outside Barnes Travel, County Road, Walton, with a good mate of mine, Jeff Winters. We had grown up together in Fazakerley so it was poignant this story should involve Jeff, as it was with Jeff I'd gone to see my first Everton match – a 3-1 victory over Swansea City at Goodison Park in 1981. Howard Kendall was player/manager that day and a certain Bob Latchford netted a consolation for the opposition.

The mood on the coach was lively, and expectancy was high. Everyone imagined we would beat Norwich City and make it to Wembley for our fourth FA Cup final in the space of just six years. People were talking about the prospects of another Merseyside final and hoping we could exact revenge for the defeat in the same competition three years previously.

By the time we'd reached Warrington on the M62, the banter was becoming more and more lively. Dozens of jokes and FA Cup trivia questions were being banded about as Blues fans geared up for the big occasion. Fans were also making their scoreline predictions but nobody could have predicted what was to happen next. The coach we were travelling on broke down and we were forced on to the hard shoulder of the motorway to wait for a replacement.

At first this apparently minor setback did nothing to dampen the spirits although, after an hour, passengers started to become concerned. It took more than an hour for another vehicle to arrive and the one that was sent to rescue us raised several eyebrows. With both Everton and Liverpool playing away in FA Cup semi-finals, every roadworthy vehicle must have been hired to ferry fans to Birmingham and Sheffield – except one.

The bus was donkeys' years old with a top speed of 30 miles per hour. Suddenly the mood had changed. Fans began to check their watches at regular intervals and the conversation had changed from whether we would win the match, to whether we would actually see any of it. Slowly but surely, fans eager to make the kick-off began to approach the driver and ask to be dropped off in order to hitchhike. Undecided as to what to do ourselves, our minds were made up for us when the bus pulled into a service station and the driver apologised for not being able to take us any further as the gearbox had 'gone' and we would have to get off. It was now every man for himself.

Stranded at a service station on the southbound carriageway on the M6, we quickly made our exits in search of a willing driver who could drop us off en route to Villa Park.

The first person we spotted was sat in a silver Citroen eating burger and chips, holding a can of orange Tango and quietly reading a newspaper.

'Let's ask him,' I said and walked over to the driver's window which was wound down.

'All right, mate, are you going past Birmingham?' I asked. The man finished taking a drink, folded his newspaper, looked up and said, 'Yes.'

Buoyed by these encouraging words, I asked, 'Is there any chance of a lift, like?' to which he replied, 'Sure.'

Unaware of our situation, the bloke carried on drinking from his can and reading his newspaper. Desperate to get to the match, he must have felt our eyes burning a hole in his newspaper as he quickly folded it again and asked, 'Oh, you want to go now?' We quickly said yes, and dived into the back seats relieved at securing a lift at our first attempt.

As the car drove away, the first thing that struck us was the passenger seat which was facing towards us. It looked a bit odd, but a lift was a lift so we made no comment and settled into the journey.

As we entered the motorway we began to explain our situation and where we were headed. Obviously we started to chat about football and the guy said he supported Fulham. I then asked him where he'd been and he explained he'd been to Manchester where he'd been filming. I was sat behind him so couldn't see his face properly but he wasn't someone I instantly recognised. I therefore assumed he was a director or producer but, in a quiet, unassuming manner he said he was an actor.

'Oh, what's your name?' I asked.

'Keith Allen,' he replied. At the time I hadn't heard of him, but Jeff had.

'Oh, you were The Yob, weren't you?' said Jeff.

'The Yob' was part of a comedy series in which he appeared with Rik Mayall and Ade Edmonson from the cult series The Young Ones.

He laughed quietly to himself and said, 'Yeah, that's right.'

Suddenly Jeff shouted, 'You're gonna get your fuckin' head kicked in!'

I quickly turned to Jeff as if to ask 'What are you doing?' but, much to my relief, Keith started to laugh. Apparently, this was his catchphrase in this programme.

Grateful for a lift, we were just expecting to get dropped off at the nearest motorway junction for Villa Park or on the hard shoulder of the M6. But Keith obviously liked us as he came off at the junction for Villa Park and carried on driving. In the back of the car we looked at each other and, without speaking, just grinned and put up our thumbs as if to say 'Get in there.'

Despite our good fortune it was looking increasingly unlikely we would make kick-off, especially as we got lost on more than one occasion and Keith had to stop and ask locals for directions. Keith was an actor with a reputation as being a hell-raiser but throughout the journey he was quiet, helpful and very unassuming.

By the time we eventually found Villa Park it was half past three and the streets outside the ground were deserted. We thanked Keith for his generosity and threw him a fiver for his troubles but he didn't want to accept it, saying, 'No, fuck off lads' so we bailed out before he could refuse.

We left the car in a hurry and we could hear the Evertonians singing so we quickly legged it round to the Holte End, the opposite side of the ground from where we had been dropped off. When we entered the ground the Blues were already winning 1-0 courtesy of Pat Nevin's goal. Although disappointed at missing it by a matter of minutes, it was a huge relief just to be there and soak up the atmosphere.

Jubilant scenes greeted the final whistle as thousands of elated fans applauded the Blues before making their way back to their transport and starting their journeys home, including us – except we didn't have any transport. After heated discussions with several drivers we managed to get on a double-decker bus chartered by Barnes Travel although we had to stand on the stairs throughout the journey.

Shortly after boarding the bus, a newsflash came over the radio stating that there had been an incident at Hillsborough and that fans had been injured. The mood after that announcement became very subdued and the anxiety increased as regular updates revealed serious injuries and even fatalities – a serious concern for many Blues who had friends and family at the opposite fixture. Nobody would have thought we had just secured a place at Wembley as the atmosphere was more consistent with relegation rather than celebration.

On arrival in Liverpool we got dropped off in Garston and, not having a clue where we were, got a bus to Childwall and then into town.

I can honestly say that neither Jeff nor myself have any vivid recollections of the actual match, probably due to what happened to us prior to the game and the events in Yorkshire that happened afterwards.

As for Keith, he is now perhaps better known as being the father of pop singer Lily Allen although he himself wrote and recorded the World Cup songs 'World in Motion' with New Order and 'Vindaloo' with Fat Les. On screen he has appeared in films such as Trainspotting and Mike Bassett England Manager and starred as the Sheriff of Nottingham in BBC1's Robin Hood.

Before the kick-off of the 1989 Cup final, Everton fans again showed why they are a special breed, joining in with Liverpool's anthem, 'You'll Never Walk Alone', in recognition of the 96 fans who had lost their lives at Hillsborough eight weeks previously. The game was seen as 'the Merseyside final' for more reasons than one and there were more acts of solidarity and togetherness shown by both sets of fans including chants of 'Merseyside, Merseyside, Merseyside'.

The game itself started with Liverpool on top and taking an early lead through John Aldridge. Liverpool continued to dominate until the dying minutes when, after many people had left the stadium, substitute Stuart McCall slid in an equaliser. The game went to extra time and again Liverpool took a very early lead. A screamer by McCall showed Everton's never-say-die attitude but they were undone once more by Liverpool's own substitute, Ian Rush. It was a disappointing end to a largely disappointing season.

The following season Everton showed some signs of improvement in the league, finishing in sixth place, but failed to make any significant progress in the FA or League Cups, being knocked out by Oldham Athletic and Nottingham Forest respectively. On the transfer front during 1989–90 Colin Harvey brought in the back-flipping winger Peter Beagrie and Everton's first overseas signing, Stefan Rehn from Sweden.

The 1990s

The 1990–91 season started in very disappointing fashion. The Blues won only one of their first ten games, ensuring the players and management were under increasing pressure. Something had to give and after an early League Cup exit, the board decided to end Colin Harvey's reign. His replacement was former boss Howard Kendall, who instantly installed Harvey as his number two. Everton's League form improved and eventually they finished ninth.

The highlight of the season beyond doubt was the epic fifth round FA Cup tie with Liverpool. Everton refused to give up and equalised a remarkable four times to take the game into a replay. Many people forget that Everton won that 1-0, courtesy of a Dave Watson goal.

The Blues did reach Wembley in 1991 yet it was not through the recognised League or FA Cup competitions but a competition devised to compensate for the English European ban – the Zenith Data Systems Cup. In the Northern semi-final of the competition Everton were to play Barnsley at Oakwell. For some reason, it proved to be the lowest attended away game for many a year.

I have not been short of invitations to other clubs and have been received more warmly by Everton than I have by Liverpool.

Bill Shankly after his retirement

Barnsley v Everton, Zenith Data Systems Cup Northern semi-final, 1991
Déjà Vu by Jimmy Smith

In 1991, I was working and living in Erdington, which is just off the M6 near Villa Park. While I was there, Everton were due to play at Barnsley. I hadn't missed a game for years but decided not to go because it was a midweek game so far away and I was living in digs.

Around 2 o'clock on the day I started to get itchy feet so decided I'd go after all. I asked the lad I was working with if he fancied going with me. The lad wasn't into football at all, but when I said, 'You can come with me or I can drop you off at our digs' he decided he'd come along as it was something to do.

Around 3 o'clock, we went back to our digs, got changed and set off on the long journey up the M42 and then M1 to Barnsley. The journey was OK despite driving all the way in an old Ford Transit van which had no radio and had seen better days.

We arrived in Barnsley to find one or two people milling about outside the ground. It didn't concern me that there weren't many people around as it was quite early and the crowds for these types of games were always low. I had been to a similar fixture against Norwich City in the Screen Sport Super Cup with around 50 other Everton supporters in 1985. I remember being outside Carrow Road before the game and one of their players, Robert Rosario, came out and gave us about 300 tickets. We sat in the pub and couldn't even give them away!

Despite it being a Mickey Mouse cup, it was an Everton game so, as always, I got that buzz you get just before a game as we parked up and made our way into the Barnsley Supporters' Club for a pint. Inside, everything looked ordinary. There were around a dozen people in there and we headed for the bar where I ordered two pints of lager. The barman recognised my Scouse accent and, pouring the drinks, asked, 'They knows game's off dun't thee?'

97

I couldn't believe it. We'd travelled for two and a half hours only to find the match had been called off! So that we didn't look stupid, quick as a flash I said, 'Oh yeah, we're just working around the corner.'

When I turned round with our drinks, I noticed the lad I was with was more gutted than me. His gob hit the floor when he heard the news as we'd gone straight to the match with no dinner and he was wishing he'd gone back to our digs.

Because there were no mobile phones in those days and our van had no radio, we had no idea the game had been cancelled so I said to the barman, as if out of curiosity, 'So what was the game called off for, anyway?'

The barman explained that the drains in the ground had somehow leaked and flooded the pitch which caused the match to be called off at around 3 o'clock. We didn't want to make it look like we had gone there just for the match so we stayed for another pint before making a sharp exit to complete our five-hour, 300-mile round trip back to Birmingham.

When the game was replayed a fortnight later on Wednesday, 13 March, I made the trip again from Birmingham. This time I made sure the game was on and got into Oakwell courtesy of free tickets I'd been given by former Everton player, Stuart Rimmer, who was on loan at Barnsley at the time. This time, we actually saw a game and left a lot happier as we won the match 1-0 thanks to a goal from Tony Cottee. What's more, we actually had something to talk about on the long drive home!

I came to Goodison as a youngster and it is something that you can't get away from. Once it is in you it's there and that's why I enjoy coming and watching as many games as I can.

Lee Trundle, Evertonfc.com, September 2006

Although Everton beat Leeds over the two legs of the Northern final, the Wembley hoodoo continued as we were embarrassed 4-1 by lowly Crystal Palace in the national final. Just like he did at the start of the season against Leeds United, Neville Southall staged a one-man protest by sitting in his goalmouth, refusing to collect his medal. Here, one Evertonian recollects that game and the antics of an uninvited Liverpool fan.

Zenith Data Systems Cup final v Crystal Palace, Wembley, 7 April 1991
The Tranny by Alan McClintock

It all started with someone's stupid idea to go to this pointless final. Drinking copious amounts of alcohol played a large part in the positive response from all concerned. Tickets purloined and so, pre-nanny state, all ten of us piled into the back of our trusty Transit with two mattresses, grub and beers. There were three of us up front sharing the driving. What's more, there were hangovers all round from the previous night's routine bash in town. That said, beers were opened at 7 a.m. – mandatory. One of the lads was a Red but still wanted to come for the laugh so we arranged to pick him up last and then hit the motorway.

We pulled up at his house and gave him the three toots on the van horn. In a flash, the bathroom window burst open and out he jumped, doing a para roll when he hit the lawn. Up he got with a 'Tada!' to reveal the Heidi wig, one of his mum's dresses, ex-army boots and a pair of boxies (thank Christ). We asked him if he was bringing anything to change into to which he replied, 'No, I'm staying like this all day.' I think he was still pissed from the night before to be honest. Not to be put off, more cans were opened and off we all went.

We eventually got there to a half-empty Wembley. It was a shame but the competition was a bit of a farce anyway. The game itself was shite but what a laugh we had. It was an absolutely marvellous day with Heidi dancing on the Wembley seats, telling the stewards to fuck off every time he was told to sit down. He even got himself on TV and the cheeky bastard even took the piss when we got beat! This was one of many times we dragged the old tranny box to Wembley or the odd quarter or semi-final or two in 'the smoke'. Luckily, the van has seen bigger and better games since that Mickey Mouse cup final.

The season's end saw Howard Kendall pull off a major signing by persuading Peter Beardsley to join Everton from Liverpool. But it was goodbye to one Everton legend. Graeme Sharp made his final appearance in 1991 having scored an unbelievable 111 league goals in his time with the Blues.

Hoping to forge a partnership with 'Beardo' was a young striker who came through the ranks at the club. But first, he had to shake off a partner of a different kind.

I'd break every bone in my body for any club I play for but I'd die for Everton.

Dave Hickson

Pre-season tour to Balsthal, Switzerland, 1991
Room Mates by Stuart Barlow

In 1990 I left Sunday amateur league football in Liverpool to sign for Everton. As a Scouser, born and bred in the city, it was a dream come true for me to be playing for one of my hometown clubs. I was actually a non-contract player at Everton for two years before I signed professionally and would often play for the A-team on a Saturday, Sherwood Park on a Sunday and then the reserves in midweek. Graham Smith, who was a massive influence on my career, had chewed the ear off Colin Harvey, the manager at the time, to give me a chance and before I knew it I was training with legends like Neville Southall,

Kevin Ratcliffe and Graeme Sharp. Within a year of signing as a pro, I had made my debut and was travelling on my first pre-season tour with the Blues.

By this time, Howard Kendall had returned to the club and it was Howard and Colin Harvey who took us to the small village of Balsthal. This region, situated in the Swiss Alps, was to be our base for approximately two weeks while we played against European opposition to gain important match fitness. It was also an opportunity for the team to get to know new players and bond together.

A couple of weeks before I was due to travel, I spoke to my best mate from Fazakerley, Tony Dunn, about the tour, telling him where we were going and who we would be playing. I didn't see him before leaving and, with no mobile phones in those days, wasn't sure if he was going to travel over. Tony was in a dead-end job with hardly any money but he still decided to make the trip along with four other Evertonians. The lads had piled into a car and travelled for more than 24 hours to Switzerland. Typically, none of them had booked a hotel – their attitude was 'Let's just go and worry about digs when we get there.'

On the second day of the tour, like lots of Blues fans, Tony had made it to Balsthal and the hotel where the Everton team were staying. I was surprised to see him and even more surprised when, on the evening before our first game, he said, 'I need a place to stay.'

As I was a local lad and new to the squad, I was taken under the wing of club captain Dave Watson, with whom I shared a room. I explained to Tony that I was rooming with the Everton captain and he couldn't have my bed. What's more, I was certain Big Dave wouldn't let him have his! But, being a mate, I agreed to ask Dave if he could stay in our room although it was only about ten-foot square. When I asked Dave if my mate could get his head down in our room, he just replied, 'Yeah, no problem.'

So, later that night, Tony was thrown a few blankets and kipped on the floor. Despite the cramped conditions, and his snoring, Tony still says it was one of the best nights of his life although I can't say it was for either me or Dave. I think the gaffer knew one of the fans had stayed with us but, knowing Howard, he probably just laughed at his audacity.

Tony left the following morning and followed us to see our first game. He was joined at the match by around a thousand or so others, at least half of whom were Blues. Everton is a massive club and its supporters are fanatical, following the team absolutely everywhere. They literally invaded Balsthal and drank dry the two pubs in the village. After each pre-season game the players would go into one of the marquees pitched near to the ground for a water or soft drink.

When we would arrive, the marquees would already be full of Evertonians. When they saw you, they would always tell you where they were going that night and ask you if you fancied joining them. Such was our amazing following abroad, the foreign players like Robert Warzycha were amazed. They couldn't understand the level of support in a foreign country for just a pre-season game.

For me in particular, it was also an amazing experience but for different reasons. While on tour, I bumped into people I knew, including a family of four brothers from Fazakerley called the McHales. Months earlier I had been playing against some of these lads in amateur matches and here I was, playing for Everton in Switzerland, sharing a room with an Everton legend and my best mate!

Throughout my time at Everton, whether playing home or away, in a friendly or competitive fixture, our support was always unbelievable. This, for a local lad like me, was something special, something I'll never forget or take for granted.

Peter Beardsley's first season in a blue shirt was impressive; he top scored for Everton with 15 league goals in 1991–92. However, the team failed to live up to expectations and rarely moved from a position in mid-table, ending up a very disappointing 12th. Unfortunately, there were no Wembley appearances; the Blues were in fact knocked out at the fourth-round stage in both cup competitions.

During an international break that season, the Toffees took the opportunity to take a trip to Sestao, Spain, for a friendly match. One special fan, who always made sure he was there to watch the Blues, regardless of where they were playing, was Gerry Foran.

Mid-season friendly v Sestao, 1991–92
Talk of the Dressing Room by Gerry Foran

My story starts over half a century ago so, as you might expect, one or two areas might be a bit sketchy. However, to the best of my knowledge, these are my memories:

I went to my first football match at the age of four, a reserve team fixture between Liverpool and Everton in 1952. I was taken by my dad, Gerard 'Gus' Foran, a former professional boxer who also appeared as a 'guest' player for Everton during World War II when many footballers were completing their National Service. Although he played as a 'guest' for Everton, he was a Red who wanted me to follow in his footsteps. Ironically, I never followed boxing and became a Blue instead, going to my first game around 1958 with my mates Alan and Manneh Brown, John McKenna and Tapah Roberts. Not long after this, I was following the Blues at home on a regular basis.

In the early '60's I continued to follow Everton at home and travelled to as many away games as my uncle Harry could take me to, missing only a few home games of the glorious 1962–63 Championship winning season. People talk about the great 1969–70 Championship winning side, which included the 'Holy Trinity' of Harvey, Kendall and Ball, but in my opinion, this team, with the likes of Roy Vernon and Alex Young, was the best.

My dad didn't always approve of me travelling to follow Everton, not because he was a Red, but because of the worry it often caused. One such incident happened in 1964 when I went to Chelsea with my mate Tapah Roberts. On the night before the game we set off at midnight from St John's Lane and arrived in London around 7.00 a.m. on the Saturday morning. For some reason though, the coach dropped us at Paddington station and we had to make our own way to Stamford Bridge. On the way we decided to visit Gina Brown, Alan and Manneh's sister. Not long after getting on the underground to get to Gina's, we lost each other, but met up at the match, which we lost 1-0.

After the game we went to Gina's for a bite to eat and set off for Paddington but got lost and missed our coach home. We managed to find Euston station and eventually arrived home at 7.00 a.m., thirty-one hours after we had set off. My dad had been walking the streets of Liverpool wondering where I was. When he eventually saw me, he told me in no uncertain terms that I wasn't going again.

Despite my Dad's concerns, I continued following Everton and from August 1965 to the 1968 Cup final, I recall travelling with Paddy Geeleher and Steve Long and missing just a handful of games home and away due to playing football for Crawford's. This was also the period I started serving my apprenticeship. Consequently, following the Blues away became more difficult but somehow I managed to do it, and keep my job, but don't ask me how.

Like most Evertonians, I idolised Alex Young and on one Friday in 1966 hitched up to Hampden Park with Paddy Geeleher to see 'The Golden Vision' and Alex 'Chico' Scott play for Scotland in a Saturday evening friendly against Portugal. We left around 5 p.m. but in those days the M6 finished just north of Preston so we had to travel along A and B roads the rest of the journey including over the hills of Shap. On the way there the heavens opened and we were soaked to the skin, so much so that the dye from my shoes turned my feet black. Eventually we made it to Hampden only to see Young substituted after just 20 minutes through injury.

Almost twenty years later, in 1985, I became a steward at Everton. My duties included looking after former chairman Sir John Moores as well as watching games at Goodison sat on top of the executive boxes. I performed my duties at one end whilst at the other end was the legendary Evertonian Eddie Cavanagh.

It was through my role as a steward that I became friendly with Howard Kendall and Colin Harvey. I got on well with both Howard and Colin when they managed Everton and both would sort me out with tickets for away games. Over time I began to share a friendship with both these Everton legends, a friendship shared through the love of Everton Football Club.

In 1992, during an international break, Everton were invited at short notice to play a friendly against Sestao, a Spanish second division outfit based in the Basque Country. Howard Kendall contacted me when the game was announced and I immediately made arrangements to travel to Spain. The cost to travel to Bilbao by plane was expensive so I ended up travelling by train, ferry and train again to San Sebastian from where I took a bus. The journey had taken me approximately 36 hours by the time I reached the Everton team's hotel. I arrived during a torrential downpour, was soaked to the skin and was stopped by hotel security. I asked for Mr Kendall and when he saw me he asked if I wanted to travel to the game on the team bus.

'Are you sure, gaffer?' I asked.

'Yeah,' said Howard. 'Help Jimmy Martin with the kit.'

So without hesitation I got changed into my Everton tracksuit to look the part and boarded the team bus along with the players and staff.

At the ground, Howard introduced me to the Sestao chairman who escorted us to the boardroom. As the chairman was about to pour me a large Scotch I said, 'No thank you.'

'You no drink?' he asked.

'Oh yes, but I prefer brandy', so he poured me a large brandy instead and we enjoyed a nice drink together. Howard could speak Spanish fluently from his time as manager of Bilbao and he began speaking the lingo, which the chairman loved.

After our drink we had a tour of the Estadio Las Llanas before heading to the dressing room. When the time came for the team talk I asked Howard if he wanted me to leave but he said I could stay. I felt a bit awkward so decided to wait outside anyway.

Outside the dressing rooms I looked at the pitch, which was under around two inches of water. The game would probably have been cancelled had it not been for the fact that Everton had travelled so far. As I was gazing around the small stadium, Everton captain Kevin Ratcliffe approached me. 'You're getting talked about in the dressing room,' he said.

Puzzled at his comments, I raised my eyebrows as if to say 'What do you mean?'

'The team talk is about you,' said Rats. 'The boss has just said you made the effort to get here so let's make an effort and put on a show for Gerry.'

Naturally I was warmed by his comments – as well as the frequent visits to the boardroom for more brandies with the chairman.

After the game, which finished 2-2, I helped Jimmy Martin collect the kit and load it on to the team bus. Howard then invited me to a suite similar to the 500 Club or Joe Mercer Suite that was situated at the back of the main stand. The Everton team were on one long table while the Sestao team were on a table opposite. 'Take a seat,' said Howard, pointing to a chair opposite Peter Beardsley and other Everton idols.

'What's going on here?' I asked.

'You're having a meal with me and the players and you're most welcome.'

I sat down to a beautiful meal, at the end of which Howard gave a speech in Spanish. After receiving warm applause from the Sestao players and staff it was time to leave. On the way out, the Everton players walked past the Sestao team's table, shaking hands with each player in turn. I was about to walk away until Howard urged me to join in the farewell.

On the bus we started to have a laugh and the players were enjoying a bit of banter. I don't know what was said by Mike Newell to Neville Southall but it resulted in Mike Newell running off the bus around the ground being hotly pursued by Big Nev.

Back at the hotel I shook Howard's hand and said, 'Cheers boss, thanks for everything.'

'Where are you going?' he asked.

'I'm going to find somewhere to stay.'

'Are you OK to stay with Jimmy?' I thought he meant Jimmy Martin the kit manager but what I didn't know was that he meant former Everton legend Jimmy Gabriel, who was there as a coach. Jimmy didn't mind me rooming with him so I stayed the night with the players at their hotel before they were due to set off to Majorca the following day.

The following morning when I woke up I thought I'd been quiet and tiptoed around the room trying not to disturb Jimmy.

As I was creeping around I heard a deep Scottish voice say, 'You don't half snore. Maybe I can get some sleep now.'

Thankfully I think he saw the funny side of it and it didn't spoil the trip of a lifetime – me, the only Everton fan to travel from England to this away game and the subject of the dressing room team talk.

Everton's most successful captain Kevin 'The Rat' Ratcliffe was the highest profile exit of the 1991–92 season. After making 359 appearances and collecting two league championships, one FA Cup and one European Cup Winners' Cup medal along the way, he left to join Cardiff City. Howard Kendall brought in a number of new names during the season including Glasgow Rangers' free scoring Scot Mo Johnston, future Wembley hero Paul Rideout and the Yugoslav Predrag Radosavljevic who became commonly known as 'Preki'.

The Blues, determined to improve on their mid-table finish, readied themselves for 1992–93 with a pre-season trip to Switzerland. Andy Nicholls, author of the book 'Scally', was one of the dedicated few who made the trip.

Pre-season friendly, Balsthal, Swizerland, 1992
The Flag of Balsthal! by Andy Nicholls

With the team doing poorly and no back door entry through the Intertoto or Fair Play League, in those days the only chance of a trip to Europe with the mighty Blues was during pre-season. Plenty took the opportunity every summer to bin off the likes of Ibiza and Benidorm to watch our beloved Everton in some outback town in the middle of nowhere!

We always took a hardcore couple of hundred to most games abroad and over the years I have watched Everton in more than 20 countries. Although the lads are often looked upon as endorsing, shall we say, 'an unsavoury element', there is no doubt that among the group are some of the most loyal supporters the club has ever seen.

Most trips have the odd 'incident' – a bit of shoplifting gone wrong, the customary drunken fallout and handbags at midnight with your best mates after disagreeing over something deadly serious like which Duncan was the best, Mackenzie or Ferguson! All in all though, most trips were an excuse to go on a jolly and sample something that our unruly neighbours were somehow lucky enough to have a taste of every year.

Anyway, back to Balsthal for pre-season. I was working in Germany at the time and had a boss who, let's say, didn't endear himself to me. He stuttered so badly that even a simple question had you covered in spit. After one such conversation I decided to jack in the job, sell a few tools and meet up with the lads on this pre-season tour of Switzerland. Twenty-four hours later the spit on my face had been swapped for a handgun and I was sorry I had ever set foot in a small town which, as predicted, was 'in the middle of nowhere!'

I had jumped a train from Frankfurt to Zurich and then got on the local network service which made the Liverpool to Wirral service look as luxurious as a top of the range trip on the Orient Express! Basically, don't believe what they say about train services abroad. Yes, main city lines are a dream, but go off the beaten track and the dream becomes a nightmare. I spent about three hours sitting in a one-carriage horse wagon of a train next to a fella who stank. Well, it was him or the goat with him; one of them did and my money was on him – the goat was cleaner! We had covered about 40 miles in this time and even by Everton's standards of going to unknown places, I had my doubts that even our penny-pinching board would send us this far into oblivion.

Then, as is always the case with Everton, the lads turned up! To the right of me, a Leasowe Van Hire sign appeared on the road running alongside the train track. Within minutes, I had pulled the cord of the slowest train in the world, said my goodbyes to the bemused passengers and the collection of animals, hopped across the track and joined the lads, who, after three days of travelling, smelled worse than the goat and/or its owner!

About an hour later, we were booked into a nice little complex with chalet-style rooms on two levels and were washed and Lynxed-up ready for a night on the lash. Things got even better when we entered the bar and saw a collection of players led by the Maverick Mo Jo Johnston propping up the said bar. He was obviously not concerned about the poor state of fitness of the squad which, the previous season, had played a major part in us once again having bugger all to play for after the second week of January! Still, who were we to complain? Sacking a few beers was hardly going to turn us into champions again, so we joined them. We had a boss night, with Mo Jo and a few others who were more than happy to allow us to tag on with them as long as we promised not to do anything daft!

In theory, it sounded a good idea; in practice it was never going to happen. At about two in the morning about twenty of us, including Mo Jo, were staggering back to the hotel when one of the lads spotted a huge blue and white flag taking pride of place in the town centre. It was a truly magnificent flag, in royal blue Everton colours with a huge snake embossed across the front of it. In a nutshell, it was made for us, and we had to have it . . . so we did!

One of the lads scaled up the flagpole and within minutes we were arguing about what slogan we were going to have across it when it was draped over the stands at the first game of the season! Once back at the hotel, we took a great team picture of it and Mo Jo was proudly at the front, a move which very nearly brought his Everton career to an end! Back in the rooms – as usual we had booked doubles but had the customary ten bunking in to keep the cost as low as possible – the remaining ale was finished off and it was goodnight, God bless, and bring on the game. I remember thinking, if I feel this bad and I only have to watch, how the fuck is Mo Jo going to play? That wasn't my problem – HK was the boss!

At about silly o'clock there was a massive bang on the door and an obvious commotion was in full swing in the hotel as all you could hear was shouting and bawling and doors slamming. I opened the door and saw an irate car-park attendant-looking fella who was ranting and raving in his incomprehensible native tongue. He demanded to see our papers and one lad made a big mistake by throwing a two-day-old copy of The Sun at him and telling him to fuck off. That was the last straw. The attendant reached into his jacket and pulled out a handgun that looked about as old as he did. All the same, it seemed real enough and capable of blowing a large hole in someone's head!

He put it against my chin and said in broken English, 'Where is the flag? That flag is the flag of Balsthal. It has been here for one hundred years and survived two World Wars. You have been here one day and my flag has gone!'

He had a point. It had indeed gone and was, in fact, in the boot of one of the lads' cars! We were marched out and a few were handcuffed while the rooms were searched. The flat-capped General then found a camera and was told by the hotel manager that we had been seen taking pictures of the flag hours earlier. Now this bloke was no Columbo, he was not even an Officer Dibble, but even he worked out that once the film was developed he would have those responsible for the theft of his town's beloved flag.

Within minutes, a sheepish-looking Mo Jo appeared and asked us to hand back the flag. It was a good idea, given the fact that the flat cap had said everyone on the photos would go directly to jail with no £200 for passing Go! It was agreed that the lad would drive the car a few yards out of the hotel grounds and sling the flag in the bushes, giving the local bizzies the satisfaction of 'finding' the said item which was obviously the pride and joy of this sad little town.

As we were still lined up outside the hotel, a taxi pulled up and out got the Legend that is Neville Southall. He was deadpan, as always, as he looked at us, handcuffed and being help at gunpoint, albeit by a crap gun and said, 'Breakfast shit was it lads?!' and walked casually into the lobby!

Minutes later there was movement outside and flat cap was radioed to attend a crime scene. An eagle-eyed PC had found the flag. He was a hero and was given funny handshakes, back slaps, hugs and kisses from his work colleagues! Within an hour, we were told to leave town, never to return, while Columbo and his gang drank whisky in the hotel bar to celebrate a job well done.

I can't even remember if we watched the game later that day. It was like that on tour: we were usually that pissed that the games were either a blur or not attended. One thing I do remember though, is that no matter what town I am in, whatever part of the world, I respect their local historical items. Robbing a two-bob flag from some dog-breath town in the middle of nowhere can be seen as very serious to their chief of police. It can be just as serious as melting down and selling the Eiffel Tower as scrap metal would be to the bloke employed in the same job in Paris!

Everton are the people's club in Liverpool. The people on the street support Everton.

David Moyes speaking on the day he joined Everton

The following season was also mediocre by Everton's standards. The Blues finished 13th, yet only four points above the relegation zone. In the cups, they again disappointed; embarrassingly knocked out of the FA Cup by the then Second Division Bolton Wanderers.

The 1992–93 season was possibly more memorable for affairs off the pitch than on it, for Everton Football Club was put up for sale at the end of the season with lifelong Evertonian Bill Kenwright and Peter Johnson in a struggle for control. Despite the unrest, the Blues still managed to bring in Graham Stuart from Chelsea in a deal worth £850,000, which was to prove to be a shrewd bit of business.

In the same year, Everton invited a young, enthusiastic Dutchman to Goodison Park.

Everton v Southampton, 19 December 1992
Dutch Courage by Michael Koeslag

I began taking an interest in Everton after watching their European heroics in 1985. I recall asking for an Everton pennant in a sports shop over here in Sittard (The Netherlands) and the owner talking fondly about the Everton supporters' behaviour in the European Cup Winners' Cup game with Fortuna Sittard during the 1985 cup run. The owner told me how friendly the Everton supporters had been, even playing footie with the police in the town square.

Also, I remember watching Everton play in the 1987 Charity Shield against Coventry on TV. After that, I kept looking out for Everton's results on teletext, as in those days there was no internet, and started supporting Everton from then onwards.

My first Everton game, as a 16-year-old, was a friendly with PSV Eindhoven in December 1990. At the game I tried to ask for autographs, but at that time, the pitch was still surrounded by high fences, so I didn't have much joy.

However, as I went back to my seat, I was approached by an Everton fan who later turned out to be my best mate, Gerry Foran. Gerry offered to send all the autographs on paper if I gave him my address. When Gerry casually put my details in his back pocket, my father tried to convince me not to get my hopes up too much.

However, a few weeks later Gerry got in touch, sending me match-day programmes. Soon afterwards, the promised autographs arrived and we started writing to each other.

Not long after this, in 1991, Gerry invited me to come over to England to watch the Blues. However, as Gerry's dad died soon before Christmas 1991, my first visit to watch the Blues was delayed until December 1992.

I flew from Holland to Manchester and was picked up at the airport by Gerry, who took me to Liverpool. Gerry had arranged for me to meet the players and sit in the directors' box for the game against Southampton – a real five-star package for my first game at Goodison Park. I remember being nervous meeting the players, but Neville Southall was a great character and Howard Kendall was very friendly.

When we left the home dressing room before the game, we saw Matt Le Tissier coming towards us. My friend Gerry quickly informed me that an English international was about to walk past us, so told me to get ready for a picture with Matt. Superstitious as I was, even at that age, I wasn't too keen to have my picture taken with an opponent, but there was not much I could do in the end.

When I took my seat just before kick-off and the Z Cars tune began to play, I got a shiver down my spine. Five minutes into the game, Neville Southall collected the ball after a Southampton attack. As he was about to throw it out, his arm hit the body of Dutch defender Ken Monkou, the ball fell loose and you guessed it, Matt Le Tissier was on hand to tap the ball into an empty net! You can imagine how shell-shocked I was in my nice seat in the directors' box.

Fortunately, the Blues turned the game around and won 2-1, thanks to goals from Paul Rideout and Peter Beardsley.

After that first visit, I came over to watch my beloved Blues, mostly at Christmas and Easter, trying to squeeze in as many home and away games as possible.

The highlight was obviously in 1995 when I was at Wembley to see Everton beat Manchester United in the FA Cup final and I was back again a few months later for the Charity Shield win over Blackburn. My brother came along to watch both games; however, he made a slight mistake for the Man Utd game as he was wearing a red jacket among 40,000 Blues. Perhaps that's where the expression 'Dutch courage' comes from!

Also, over the years, I have managed to see Everton in various pre-season games in Germany (1992, 1993 and 1994), Holland/Belgium (1998), the south of England (2000), Austria (2002) and Scotland (2003).

The best of these was obviously the tour in Belgium and Holland; the most memorable game being a 6-1 win over amateur side VV Una. Most of the Evertonians had spent the game watching from the terrace of the local sports canteen, drinking beer, sponsored kindly by manager Walter Smith apparently.

After the game a few of those Everton fans got on to the pitch for a kickabout. Even now, my friend Gerry still recalls the sight of those drunken Everton fans trying to get on to the end of some delightful crosses delivered by my sister Monique!

Over the years I have met lots of Blues fans at the games and they always make me more than welcome. I was officially adopted as a Scouser on my 30th birthday when, on another trip over with my girlfriend, my mother and mother-in-law, my Everton friend Tommy came knocking on the door of the F1 Hotel. Tommy had a touching birthday card for me with the words: 'To an adopted Scouser, happy 30th birthday.' That's what's special about Everton supporters: they are genuinely friendly and have a passion for their team which is infectious. The term 'People's Club' couldn't be more appropriate.

Since his first game in 1990, Michael has followed Everton home and away in each successive season since. He even managed to appear in Dave Prentice's column in the Liverpool Echo which reported Michael's impressive performances in the Dutch version of 'Fantasy Football'.

His loyalty to Everton was also demonstrated when he had an article published in Dutch football magazine Voetbal International, in which he voiced his objections to Duncan Ferguson's punishment by the Scottish FA in comparison to Patrick Kluivert's community service received for killing a person after drink-driving.

As an Evertonian, Michael has witnessed some highs and lows. Despite the lows, like a true Blue, he remains as loyal as ever.

For Everton's end-of-season tour, the exotic choice was Mauritius and, as usual, Gerry Foran was there.

End of season tournament, Mauritius, 1993
Everton's New 44-year-old 'keeper by Gerry Foran

At the end of the 1993 season, Howard Kendall called me to his office at Bellefield. When I arrived at his office he informed me that Everton had been invited to Mauritius to play in an end-of-season tournament along with Aston Villa and a representative team from the island. He asked me not to share this information with anyone as it was a last-minute job and the club wanted it kept low key.

'I'll have to tell one person,' I said. 'I'll have to tell Tommy Ennis, because I travel everywhere with him.'

For a few years we'd followed Everton home and abroad, experiencing many laughs as well as one or two scary moments. In 1989, after watching Everton play PSV Eindhoven, the ferry we were travelling back home on sailed into a hurricane. This significantly delayed our return but didn't stop us turning up at Goodison Park later that evening for a reserve team fixture. Our presence at the game was even noted by Colin Harvey, who shook his head in disbelief, saying, 'There's something wrong with you two!'

On another occasion, we travelled to a mid-season friendly in Derry, Northern Ireland. We had flown over and hired a car during 'the troubles' and our car was stopped and searched at a bridge crossing. The soldier who stopped us recognised our accents as he was a Scouser himself. It was only after the match, when we learnt that five bombs had been found and defused that day, that the reality of the situation hit home, proving it's never dull watching Everton – even in a friendly.

Over the years we've experienced a few bumpy rides, one of which happened during a visit to Spain to watch Everton play Athletic Bilbao. We landed heavily in Spain, and later discovered it was because our plane's undercarriage had collapsed on landing. Fortunately our duty frees weren't damaged and we travelled to Bilbao to meet Howard Kendall, who gave us five tickets for the game. After twenty-eight of us managed to get in with these five tickets, we went out for a drink in the town. Howard told us to wear Basque berets to impress the locals and it did as they bought us a few beers.

Howard agreed to me telling Tommy, but as it was expensive and such short notice he couldn't make it to Mauritius and, as I was due to go away myself, neither could I.

A few days later I was working in my cab when I got a call asking me to go to my mum's house but not to panic. When I got there my mum asked me to work out how much she had won on a five-horse accumulator. When I totalled it up she had won £5,800, of which she kindly gave me £1,500 – enough to get me to Mauritius. Howard was pleased when he heard I was going and told me he'd sort me out if I needed anything when I was over there.

Before I knew it I was on my way to Mauritius via Euston, Heathrow, Paris, Réunion Island, which is the sister island of Mauritius, and then eventually Mauritius itself. In total it took around 24 hours before I arrived at the players' hotel.

Once there, I asked, as on similar occasions, to speak to Howard Kendall. Howard greeted me and I joined the players as they watched the FA Cup final between Arsenal and Sheffield Wednesday. I enquired about the accommodation at the hotel but when I discovered that staying there would set me back £137 per night, I quickly decided to look elsewhere. I eventually found a less expensive establishment at a fraction of the price – £8 per night – a bargain with its own corrugated roof above my room and free lizard in the wardrobe.

I stayed there and in the morning went back to the players' hotel. A lot of the players such as Stuart Barlow and Ian Snodin were good to me, as was Jimmy Gabriel, who I'd roomed with in Sestao, as well as the coach Dave Fogg, who let me shower in his room as mine never had one.

A couple of days into the tour, an impromptu seven-a-side game between Everton staff and the hotel staff was arranged. Howard knew of the game and approached me at the bar while I was having a drink.

'Go and represent your team,' he said, asking me to play.

'I've just got this pint,' I said.

'Don't worry about that, I'll take care of that for you.' And so off I went to join the Everton staff.

I met with the Everton team which included Peter Beardsley, Gary Ablett, Neil Moore, John Doolan, Jimmy, the kit man, and Ian Irving, the club doctor. Peter Beardsley took charge of the team and immediately spotted my potential by putting me between the posts. The game itself was a one-sided affair with Beardsley weaving his usual magic. He struck a sweet volley right into the face of the hotel team's keeper, who took the full force without making a murmur. Peter went over to see if he was OK and he just nodded. I remember thinking, 'He's brave, he never said a word.'

Later that night in the hotel bar, the keeper who played for the hotel team approached me and tugged at the Everton pin on my shirt. It was then I realised that he was mute, so no wonder he never complained about a Peter Beardsley thunderbolt! Naturally I handed over my pin to help ease the pain of defeat and Beardo's volley.

I was enjoying life on the island and travelled to the first game of the tournament against Aston Villa. During the game, which we were unfortunate to lose 3-1, I was sat by the team bench although on this occasion, for some reason, Howard didn't ask me to represent my team.

I travelled back on the team bus and the following day I was enjoying a quiet drink at the bar in the hotel when one of the players came over to me. To my surprise he questioned my presence as I was a fan and not a member of staff. I was gutted by his comments, so moved away to a quiet spot at the bar. A few moments later someone approached me and told me that Howard wanted a word with me, so I called in on Howard who was in his room at the time.

When I sat down he looked at me and said, 'I know.'

'What do you mean?' I said.

'I know what was said and I want you to know I'm upset about it but I have to also think of the players.'

Howard offered me a drink to help wash away the bad taste from my mouth and we sat together trying to put Everton to rights. It was during our conversation that Howard told me he had to sell our star player Peter Beardsley. I didn't know what was more disappointing, having my presence questioned by a player or being told we were having to sell the crown jewels.

When the next game against Mauritius came around I was once again asked to travel on the team bus. Howard asked me to help Jimmy Martin with the kit and as we were going into the ground we were greeted by autograph hunters. When they came to me for my autograph I tried to explain I wasn't an Everton player but Colin Harvey shouted over, 'Just sign the autograph!' so I did.

The match was attended by the Prime Minister of Mauritius, who arrived at the ground accompanied by five bodyguards. Howard took the liberty of introducing me to him and he seemed impressed by the fact I was an Everton fan who had travelled to an island off the coast of the African continent over 500 miles east of Madagascar. We won the game 3-0 which, along with meeting the Prime Minister, finished the holiday off on a high note for me.

At the end of the week, on the Saturday morning, I travelled back to England via Riyadh, Saudi Arabia, where I was delayed for four hours. The players left well after me but we met up again at Heathrow airport from where I headed back to Liverpool. Despite the one sour note, all in all it was a good holiday, made special for me by Howard Kendall who, when manager of Everton, always made a fuss of me wherever I went.

It is through his love for Everton that Gerry developed friendships with influential Everton figures including Howard Kendall and chairman Bill Kenwright. Two moments illustrate just how highly he is thought of by the two.

Gerry kept in touch with Howard Kendall when Howard moved to Greece to manage Greek side Xanthi. Gerry and his partner Pam, who was pregnant at the time, made the journey to see the former Everton boss. On arrival they were faced with a lengthy car journey to where Howard was based.

Howard was overwhelmed by Gerry's efforts and insisted he stayed the night at his club-owned apartment. Gerry and Howard remained in contact with each other throughout Howard's managerial travels and they remain friends today.

When Everton played Plymouth Argyle in an FA Cup tie in January 2008, the game was televised live, which meant kick-off time was rearranged for early evening. A friend of Gerry's couldn't make it because of the late kick-off so asked Gerry to try and get back the money he paid for the three tickets he'd bought. Gerry, always willing to help out a fellow Evertonian, tried to sell his tickets outside the ground at face value. After he had sold one, a steward informed the police. Gerry protested his innocence, saying he was making no profit from selling the tickets, but the police lifted him, forcing him to miss the game. Unbeknown to Gerry and most fans, the law states that a ticket cannot be sold at any price in the vicinity of the ground on match day as doing so constitutes touting.

Gerry eventually left the police cells at 1.00 a.m. the following morning and requested to attend court to have his case heard. Devastated at the possibility of receiving a three-year Home Office ban from visiting football grounds, Gerry began the long journey home.

Once home, he contacted Bill Kenwright to explain what had happened. Knowing Gerry was a loyal supporter and of good character, Bill immediately offered to pay for his legal representation and contacted a solicitor on his behalf.

When the case came before the court, Bill Kenwright provided the magistrates with a glowing reference for Gerry, who also received a reference from former Everton secretary Michael Dunford, who was working for Plymouth at the time.

The magistrates took into account the references before passing a not-guilty verdict on a case that should never have gone to court. On leaving the court, one of the magistrates commented to Gerry that he had 'friends in high places'.

On leaving court, Gerry immediately phoned Bill Kenwright, as Bill had insisted he contact him as soon as the verdict was announced. Bill was delighted with the news and, with justice finally done, Gerry was able to continue to watch his beloved Blues.

As Gerry's story reveals, Peter Beardsley was sold at the end of the 1992–93 season. During his short stay (95 appearances in total) he became a firm favourite at Goodison Park. Despite being the wrong side of 30, Beardsley displayed some mesmerising skills and intelligent play during a period at Everton when these qualities were distinctly lacking.

Although the crowd favourite had left, Everton started the new season very brightly, winning the first three games. However, in December, Howard Kendall approached the board to fund the signing of Dion Dublin from Manchester United and they refused. Kendall, not prepared to work with his hands tied, resigned immediately.

Norwich manager Mike Walker took over as Everton boss in the new year and set about trying to turn Everton's fortunes around with some quick signings. Anders Limpar, Joe Parkinson and Brett Angell were brought in but the team struggled to put decent results together. A wretched run of form that saw seven defeats from ten games ensured that the Blues went into the last game of the season needing to win to retain their top-flight status, which had been maintained since 1954.

Wimbledon, Everton's opponents, were the surprise team that season and they took an early two-goal lead. It didn't look good. Anders Limpar was adjudged to have been fouled in the area soon after and Graham Stuart coolly converted the penalty. Deep into the second half, and still needing two goals to stay up, Barry Horne lashed a 30-yard shot that curled like a banana into the corner of the net to make the score 2-2. Eight minutes before the end, Graham Stuart popped up with the winner and the Evertonians went wild. At the final whistle, fans invaded the pitch and the joy and relief was there for all to see. This exemplified how important it was to stay in the top flight but also how, alarmingly, Everton's standards had slipped.

Everyone involved with the club was keen to avoid a repeat performance in the 1994–95 season. Peter Johnson eventually won control of the club and provided Mike Walker with cash to spend. In came Nigeria's World Cup star Daniel Amokachi, a £3 million deal, and neat midfielder Vinnie Samways from Tottenham Hotspur.

Unfortunately, Everton continued in the same vein as they had finished the previous season. Their first win, a tight 1-0 victory against West Ham United, came as late as November and they made the worst start to a season in their history. Soon after, Mike Walker was sacked, incidentally just before a massively important Merseyside derby.

The board hired the very pop ular Joe Royle to take charge. Joe could not have chosen a bigger game to make his managerial debut for his boyhood club. Here, the former Blues boss describes events that November evening in 1994.

At Everton it was special. People talk about the quality of Premier League football now but I really do believe that side could've held their own with anybody that's around today.

Andy Gray, Autobiography

Everton v Liverpool November 21 1994
My first game as manager by Joe Royle

One great occasion for me was my first game back as manager when we played Liverpool at Goodison and we beat them 2-0 when we weren't supposed to. They were 1-4 on with the bookmakers, who gave us no chance. We were bottom of the table with eight points from 14 games and I think they were riding high at the top of the league. So it was billed as the massacre of all massacres. After the game and a terrific victory in front of the Goodison crowd I was in the directors' box with the chairman and my wife enjoying the win. Then there was a knock on the door. It was one of the stewards saying that the landlord of the Winslow pub on Goodison Road wanted to speak to me. So I went out to speak to him and he said, 'Joe, do us a favour, can you pop into the pub before you leave because the supporters won't go – I can't close the place because they won't leave.' So it was past closing time when I went down and the place was absolutely rocking. I went in and it just went wild.

Paul Rideout scored the winner that night but it was the scorer of the first goal who was to become the Gwladys Street's new hero. Duncan Ferguson was initially on loan from Glasgow Rangers and the Goodison faithful immediately fell for his all-action style, his never-say-die-attitude and his aggressive nature.

Joe Royle turned Everton's fortunes that season and instilled the now famous 'dogs of war' mentality. Every player fought for the cause and gave one hundred per cent. Their form from the derby onwards ensured they secured their Premiership status in the penultimate game of the season. Here, Joe recalls how the humour of the Everton fans was always a big factor, especially at away matches.

Everton v Queens Park Rangers, 18 March 1995
Off, Off, Off by Joe Royle

In March 1995 we had an away game against Queens Park Rangers. We weren't guaranteed safety at this stage of the season. In fact, we secured safety only in the second to last game of the season at Ipswich. We'd had a fantastic run to reach the position we were in given the start we'd had to the season. Our form after winning the Merseyside derby, if extended over the season, would have seen us finish sixth or seventh. We'd just gone off like a train. However, for all our good results, due to the poor start we had, we were technically still not safe and we had to keep that run going. The Queens Park Rangers game was a tricky one because they were down there as well – it was a real relegation battle.

We always travelled well so I would say there were about four thousand Evertonians at Loftus Road. At the time we were also in the middle of a very good cup run and had just beaten Newcastle in the quarter-final the previous week to make it through to the semi-final. The interest was there and the fans were keen to see it through.

The travelling fans always gave us an unbelievable reception; they are your hardcore fans. They are the fans that go every week and live and breathe the club. They're the type of fans who will go down to Loftus Road on a freezing cold day and still be keen. The facilities there aren't that fantastic and they're not going to have great seats and they know that. So in many ways the away fans are the best fans.

Big Brett Angell, bless him, had been doing very well in training, trying his best, which he always did. I was well aware that he wasn't particularly popular with the Everton fans who'd seen snippets of him under Mike Walker. That said, I'd decided to give him a run and see how it went. Added to that, Daniel Amokachi hadn't been scoring freely – so it made sense. So we were at Loftus Road, which is a tight pitch, which looking back maybe didn't suit Brett, but he had to have his chance. With all that in mind, we really needed to win so I put him in.

It just seems like yesterday – I can remember it so clearly. It was after just a few minutes and Brett fouled somebody – really clattered into him. He was always aggressive and honest, but to be fair it was late and he deservedly got booked. About ten or fifteen minutes later he clattered into somebody again. At this point I was very aware that the crowd were shouting, 'Off, off, off!' I looked up and saw it was the Everton fans! It was very cruel because Brett's a nice man and had always tried hard and done his best wherever he's been. So determined was he to do well for Everton that he actually tried to run off a broken ankle in a reserve game. He was a real good pro but the Evertonians just never took to him, which was a shame.

I made the decision to take him off at half-time as we were 1-0 down. I brought on Daniel Amokachi to replace him and we eventually won the game 3-2 with a last-minute Andy Hinchcliffe free kick. What a winner it was. Andy, who played such a part in our revival and was actually thinking of retiring when I first came to the club, curled it right into the postage stamp in the corner of the net. I'll always remember his celebration – he just walked away as if nothing had happened!

The atmosphere at the end when we won was terrific, especially in London. It reminds me of when we used to come back from London as players; myself, Colin, Brian Labone and Bally and the rest. There was no better feeling. And we used to get the same train home as the fans back then so you'd get supporters coming through the carriages wanting to congratulate you and chat about the match.

I will never, ever forget the Everton fans. The support I have received from the people of Liverpool is special. Everton fans are part of my blood because of the way they have stood by me. Their loyalty to me is one of the main reasons why I love Everton so much.

Duncan Ferguson

Royle's first season, however, will not only be remembered for the remarkable turnaround he produced but also the fabulous FA Cup run that culminated in Everton's first Wembley appearance since the 1980s. During the cup run, Everton produced some great football, most notably in the semi-final at Elland Road when they beat Tottenham Hotspur 4-1, playing them off the park. For Joe this was one of his finest hours.

> For me the league was always more important than the cup. I'd inherited a team in a bad position but I'd never want to be remembered as the manager who was relegated with Everton. The FA Cup was just the icing on the cake.
>
> During the semi-final I told Daniel Amokachi to get warmed up because on the far side Paul Rideout had gone down injured. So I was waiting for Les Helm, the physio, to give me a message on the intercom to let me know if Rideout could go on. Dan was a great lad but I'm not sure he always understood you. He wandered over to the linesman and just put himself on!
>
> Then there's me running out of the dugout, shouting for him to come back but it was too late: he was already on. Rideout was off the pitch and whether or not he could carry on didn't matter. Dan put himself on and scored two goals. I've always said it's the best substitution I never made!
>
> I think he could have actually scored four in the half-hour he was on the field. But that was Dan for you; he could go past four or five players like they didn't exist, find himself four yards from goal and then miss the target. He was never a clinical finisher but he was a strong, powerful boy and he caused problems. So much so that I very nearly signed him years later for Man City but for a recurring knee injury. But he was a lovely boy, Dan.

As Everton were now safe, the final league game of the Premiership, away at Coventry City, was relatively insignificant. It was, however, a chance for the Evertonians to see off their heroes and wish them well for the final.

Coventry v Everton, 14 May 1995
Pitch Invaders by Simon Dougherty

I was 17 at the time and drove down to Coventry with my three mates, Scotty, Jamie and Adam, in a rusty old VW Polo. I remember listening to the 'All Together Now' '95 Cup final song on repeat, drinking Colt 45 in the back, while Jamie drove, battling the M6 towards the midlands. The game was on the last day of the season and all fans were excited in the knowledge that we were going to watch the Blues in the Cup final at Wembley the following week. Surely, today was going to be a good day.

The game itself was poor. The match ended goalless, the only highlights of the dull encounter being Anders Limpar hitting the bar and Big Nev pulling off a great save from Dion Dublin. With obviously nothing to play for in the league, and players wanting to stay injury free for the final, it was a mediocre runout to say the least.

When the final whistle blew, the pitch was invaded by Coventry fans trying to get some turf for their own back gardens and any kit from the Coventry players. A game of mob football also broke out when a ball was kicked among the hundreds on the pitch. With no referee or rules, it was every man for himself with us all wanting to run and shoot at goal. It seems strange but there didn't seem to be a big presence of police or stewards. The one steward trying to keep the peace was told to 'F*** off!' when he ordered a burly Coventry fan to please make his way out of the ground. 'You wouldn't get that behaviour at Goodison,' I thought!

My mates and I decided we'd hang about and see the Everton players on the coach and wish them good luck for the final. After waiting around for an hour and after getting the thumbs up from Daniel 'AMO, AMO', we said goodbye to the 'dogs of war'. Adam suggested we waited to say hello to former Evertonian David Burrows, then at Coventry, as he knew him personally through his dad who had sorted out his club car when he played for Everton.

As the only Evertonians remaining, we mingled amongst the Coventry autograph hunters. When Coventry player John Williams came out of the players' exit, a swarm of fans put shirts and programmes under his nose for him to sign. He looked very pleased with himself, grinning, as if to say, 'I'm the man,' until Adam shouted, 'Oi, Williams' to attract his attention. Expecting to see another adoring fan, Williams looked up only to hear Adam shout, 'You're shit!' We all pissed ourselves laughing and poor Williams just turned away.

After a brief chat with David Burrows we decided to go back. We had to walk around the outside of Highfield Road to head back to the car and it was en route that Scotty noticed a door had been left open. We looked through and, unbelievably, it gave us access back into the ground. With the stadium completely deserted, we made our way on to the pitch where we'd played mob football. With no ball to play with we improvised. Adam (a left footer), pretended to be Andy Hinchcliffe, whipping it in for me (the tallest of us) imitating my hero, Big Dunc. Celebrating a classic diving header, I ran off, sliding on my knees on the already trampled pitch. Scotty and Jamie just looked on in disbelief. Before I had time to take off my shirt and flex my biceps to the imaginary adoring fans, ten stewards appeared from nowhere. They started shouting at us before giving chase so we legged it into the stands and hid in a Ladbrokes stall. When the coast was clear we covertly made our way to the exit, taking with us great memories and over a hundred free Ladbrokes pens wedged into our pockets!

What a great away day and the best was yet to come.

I made my debut at Goodison against Stoke and was standing in the tunnel waiting to go onto the pitch. Z Cars started playing on the PA and I heard the crowd roar. If I could bottle a moment and save it for ever, then that would be it.

Alan Harper

The press were denied their dream final of Tottenham and Manchester United. Huge Evertonians Steve Samut-Tagliaferro and Ray Parr were just some of the fans who made the trip to Wembley.

FA Cup Final, Everton v Manchester United, 20 May 1995
By Royle Command by Steve Samut-Tagliaferro

I think I inherited my love for football from my father. He was a colonel in the British Army and a keen follower of both Arsenal and England. However, growing up in Malta, I began to show a keen interest in Everton and when I was nine, my dad took me to my first Everton match – the 1968 FA Cup final against West Bromwich Albion. I remember little about the game as I was overwhelmed by the whole occasion. One thing I do remember, though, is that despite the result, after watching the Blues play, it was only ever going to be Everton for me.

I have been a season ticket holder at Everton for many years now and, with Malta a three-and-a-half-hour flight away, can humbly say I am probably one of the most active supporters from abroad.

I am fortunate to be a very good friend of Howard Kendall, who has visited me here on the island. I met Howard following a bizarre series of events while on a skiing trip to Switzerland. A friend I was skiing with collided with another man, pushing him down the slope. The man swore in a broad Scouse accent as he tumbled. Recognising the accent, I went over to offer some assistance. I asked the fallen skier if he was a Red or a Blue. When he said he was a Red, I told him to pick himself up! Anyway, we made friends and he introduced me to a Blue friend of his, Ray Parr. I call Ray the 'King of Liverpool' as everyone knows him. Ray is a very good friend of Howard Kendall and it was Ray who introduced me to Howard. It was also because of Ray that I found myself on the top table at a function with the Everton team after their success in 1985. During the event, people were asking who I was so Howard introduced me as the Lord Mayor of Malta!

In 1995, I was fortunate to get a ticket from Ray Parr for the final against Man United. Delighted to be going to Wembley again, I booked on to a chartered flight with the Man United Supporters' club based over here. Most of Malta supports teams like Man United, Chelsea or the Reds. The rest support the Italian clubs. This is because Malta was a British colony so the nationalists are usually against anything British. Anyway, being the only Blue on a plane full of Man United fans, you can imagine my reception on the outward flight to London. Naturally, I took a lot of abuse but, like a true Blue, held my ground. This continued in the hotel I stayed at which again was pure red. The flak continued, but I remained quietly confident.

I met Ray at Wembley on the morning of the game and he managed to get us into a VIP area at the Hilton hotel before kick-off. I was introduced to former Everton legends, including the great Alan Ball. We got talking about Malta. He said he had a soft spot for the island as he had played there. He mentioned a Maltese player called Joe Cini and asked me to say hello to him. I was in awe of the great man – what a way to start cup final day!

The scenes at the final whistle were amazing. I particularly enjoyed the chants 'You're shit and you won fuck all' and 'Always look on the bright side of life,' which rang out for many minutes after the team's celebrations had ended.

I also enjoyed going back to the hotel bar and seeing all those miserable red faces.

The flight back to Malta was also fantastic. After taking much stick on the outward fight, the return was a different story. There was no red to be seen at all, just a blue rosette worn by the only Evertonian on board, who had plenty about which to be proud.

It's hard to explain my love for Everton to people in Malta. If I'm not at the match, I'll be listening – whatever it takes. I was once attending mass at a family wedding on a day that Everton were playing. So I ordered a taxi to pick me up during the ceremony about five minutes before the Blues were due to kick off so I could get to a TV set and watch my beloved Everton. When the family replayed the wedding video, I could be seen in the background checking my watch at regular intervals before sloping off when the taxi driver came into the church.

Over the years I have owned several yachts – 'Blue Nose', 'Toffee Girl' and my present one, 'Toffee Lady'. Each time I anchor the yacht I display code flags. If anyone was to decipher these flags, they would notice they read 'Kopites are gobshites'!

On one occasion, I was helping to deliver a small sailing yacht from Marseille to Malta. Everton were playing Newcastle so I was listening to the game on the BBC World Service programme Sportsworld. As it was only a short-wave radio, I had to hang on the side of the boat in heavy rain and a force seven gale to hear the final whistle and Everton lose 3-0. Despite the result, I impressed the three other people on board the yacht that day. At least they know what it means to be an Evertonian!

Finally, I am from a small family and all my relatives have letters such as MBE or MD listed after their names in the phone book. One day, a lady from the phone directory contacted me and asked if I had any letters I would like to have after my name in the book. I told her I did and asked her to put EFC after my name, which she did. When the lady asked what it represented, I explained it was a 'Royle' title!

Amo's Wedding by Ray Parr

After the semi-final victory over Spurs, I made arrangements for a group of Evertonians I knew from the Formby/Southport area to travel down to Wembley. I booked a brand new, never-before-used, executive coach, complete with hostess, bar and karaoke to pick us up in Formby at 7.30 on the morning of the final. As I was organising the trip, I got there 15 minutes early to check everything was OK.

When I boarded the coach I was greeted by six lads who were sat relaxing, looking very happy, nestling into the luxury seats. I recognised a couple of them, and asked what they were doing on our bus.

'We've booked a coach from the Lighthouse pub to take us to Wembley,' came the reply.

'Sorry lads, this isn't your coach, this has been booked for us.'

Just as I was explaining this, an old wreck of a bus that was falling to bits crawled around the corner and parked up at the Lighthouse. The looks of happiness and contentment were soon gone as they trudged over the road.

The rightful occupants soon set off to London, although when we arrived we parked up at Harrow and got the tube to Wembley Central.

I always liked to go to the Hilton hotel just outside Wembley Stadium for a drink before a Cup final, so, as we had a couple of hours spare, I suggested to a few of the group that we went there. But, as we approached the hotel, you couldn't get near the place. It was congested with people and you needed a pass to gain entry. Not to be deterred by this minor setback, we made our way round the back of the hotel, walked in through the service entrance, up the service lift, across into the normal lift and down into the hotel.

Once inside, we spotted a free buffet and I thought, 'That'll do us.' To be sociable, we helped ourselves to food and drinks that were on offer before heading off to watch the game.

The Cup final was a great occasion and afterwards, to celebrate, we returned to the Hilton the way we had gained entry hours earlier. As we were enjoying some more complimentary drinks I noticed none other than Everton's Neville Southall. I knew Neville and other players from my time as chairman of Kevin Ratcliffe's and Graeme Sharp's testimonial committees.

Neville was sitting quietly in a corner of the restaurant enjoying a meal with his family when I went over to speak to him.

'All right Nev, why aren't you out with the other players?' I asked.

'I'm just enjoying a meal with my family before going back to Llandudno,' said Big Nev.

I think that typified the big man's humble nature and what he had achieved in the game. As the rest of the players were celebrating

Everton's finest hour in a decade, Everton's greatest ever goalkeeper, and man-of-the-match that day, was quite happy to take the occasion in his stride, out of the spotlight with his family.

We left Nev to enjoy the evening and after a few more drinks set off to get the tube. The tube we caught back to Harrow went straight past our station without stopping so it was some time before we finally arrived back at our coach and set off.

On the motorway, as we drank and sang, we cruised past the Lighthouse bus that was making slow progress. The looks of 'what might have been' etched on to their faces as we sailed past were a picture, although the victory over Man United must surely have eased some of the pain of their journey home.

Almost immediately after the '95 Cup final, Daniel Amokachi left the UK to get married. Amo had given the Everton players and me invitations to his wedding, which was taking place in Tunisia, but most of the players were on their end-of-season holidays and so couldn't attend.

One evening, shortly after the final, I was having dinner with Duncan Ferguson and we started talking about Amo's wedding. During our conversation, and after a few more scoops, Big Dunc said, 'Do you fancy going over, you know, just for a weekend jolly?'

I thought about it and said, 'Yeah, OK' so off we went to Tunisia along with another lad, Steven Downing.

We flew to Tunisia and stayed at a very nice hotel. The following morning the three of us were sat at the bar in the middle of the hotel pool, just dangling our feet in the water. We were enjoying a few drinks when two Tunisian guys arrived. They were obviously important people as the hotel staff were giving them the VIP treatment, bowing, curtseying and so on. These guys sat next to us so we offered them a drink. I had a bottle of Bacardi; Duncan had a bottle of Scotch so it wasn't long before these lads were well on their way. During our conversations, one of the Tunisians asked if Steven was ok because he wasn't drinking. I told him Steven had picked up a stomach bug and wasn't feeling too well. On hearing this, he said to Steven, 'Come with me, I'll get you treated.'

He took Steven away and when they returned about an hour later, Steven was lost for words. I asked him what was up and he said, 'He's a prince and the other fella's his son.'

The prince had taken Steven to his palatial home and called his in-house doctor, who gave him some tablets which sorted him out.

The prince then asked 'What are you doing tonight?'

'Oh, we've got no plans like,' I said.

'Right, we're taking you out.'

Steven went to bed to recover, so Big Dunc and myself went out with the prince and his son on a pub crawl around the town of Gammarth.

The following day was Amo's wedding. Amo didn't know we were there so it was a case of surprising him.

We had a few scoops at the hotel before setting off, but when we arrived at the hotel where the ceremony was being held, we realised there was no booze as Amo's wife was a Muslim. The reception was held around the hotel swimming pool and Amo and his new wife were sat on two large thrones like a king and queen, accepting guests as they walked by. When he saw we'd made the trip over, Amo was delighted and quickly escorted us to a room away from the reception where we were treated to champagne.

We enjoyed a good night with Amo and his wife, after which he said that both his new bride, himself and some of his family were going to a famous nightclub in the middle of the desert the following night and he asked if we would like to join them.

The next night, around 7 o'clock, Amo picked Big Dunc and me up. It took around two hours to get to the club, which was in a remote part of the desert.

We eventually arrived and were enjoying a few drinks when suddenly I heard a voice say, 'Hello Ray, what are you doing here?' When I heard that, I thought, 'Who the hell could know me out here in the middle of the desert?' As I looked round, I saw Pete Price, the comedian and presenter, who enjoyed a drink with us.

Overall I enjoyed a real 'Royle' weekend, celebrating with Tunisian princes and two of Everton's FA Cup winning kings!

Every time I score, the passion comes out and I try to relay that back to the fans and to the players and the staff at how grateful I am to be playing for such a good football club. I am part of the furniture at Everton but I don't take it for granted. No money in this world could convince me to play for Liverpool. It's respect for the Everton supporters. You just can't do that. It goes against everything I stand for. Once you've played for Everton and know what it means to be a Blue then you know what it means to beat Liverpool.

Tim Cahill, Sport and Style, April 2009

A couple of years after Everton's 1995 FA Cup triumph, Ray became disillusioned at paying over the odds to look out on to Goodison Park through the glass screen of a corporate box, so purchased a terraced house near the ground, which became 'Strikers Suite'. He converted the upstairs into a flat to house a tenant to look after the place and transformed downstairs into an area for members to relax, enjoy drinks and a two-course meal cooked by the resident chef on match days. At the head of a long dining table is a large, brown leather chair which once belonged to Everton's then chairman John Moores and so sports the Everton crest. Numerous signed photographs of players such as Gary Lineker and Andy Gray hang proudly on the walls. 'Strikers Suite' is a popular destination for many former Everton heroes and has been visited by, among others, Joe Royle, Derek Temple and Alex Young. Howard Kendall can also be found there at most home games.

One evening, after a midweek televised match at Goodison, Peter Reid, covering the match for Sky TV, offered to take presenter Jeff Stelling for a drink after recording had finished. Jeff thought he was going to one of the corporate boxes but Peter took him to Strikers instead. As he was being led to a terraced house, Stelling thought it was a wind-up and he was being taken to a 'knocking shop'. When he arrived and saw the place, he was so impressed that he sent a Sky Sports news crew over the following week to report on the 'Everton house'.

The Cup final was billed as glamorous favourites against the 'underdogs of war'. With the score at 0-0, a breakaway counter attack saw Matt Jackson square the ball for the hero of '93, Graham Stuart, who just needed to slot home. However, he struck the bar with his effort. Luckily the rebound was nodded in by Paul Rideout.

The Blues held on to the 1-0 lead with superb performances from Dave Watson and Neville Southall, who ensured that the Blues rearguard would not be penetrated. Once again, more than ten years on, Everton were the Kings of Wembley.

Memorable scenes from the final saw big Duncan Ferguson, wearing a blue nose and jumping around like a man possessed, and Daniel Amokachi doing an African dance. It was an excellent day; so much so that in an interview later on that day Joe Royle described himself as 'Happy as a dog with two dicks!'

The long, drawn-out record transfer of Ukrainian speed-merchant Andrei Kanchelskis was the story of the summer of '95. This season also saw the Blues return to European competition in the Cup Winners' Cup. However, there was to be no repeat of the heroics of 1985 and, in a slightly disappointing European campaign, the Toffees were knocked out by Feyenoord.

There could be only one cure for the Blues' European exit – a derby day victory to salvage some much-needed pride.

I would love to go back because Everton are a club that will always hold a special place in my heart – once you have played for them, you will never forget what they mean.

Lee Carsley, Liverpool Echo, January 2009

Liverpool v Everton, 18 November 1995
The 'Kop Steward' by Andrew Owens

Like many Evertonians, I was taken to my first game as a young boy by my dad. It was a League Cup tie against Wimbledon at Goodison Park, which we won 8-0 thanks to Martin Dobson and Bob Latchford who scored hat-tricks. I went to the game dressed in my Everton kit with the classic Umbro diamonds running down the sleeves, although later on, I mostly wore goalie kits as my favourite player was Georgie Wood.

I definitely caught the Everton bug that day and went to as many games as I could. By 1983, I was going to more or less every game and soon afterwards became a season ticket holder during the glory days of the 1980s.

In 1995, I was on strike with the Liverpool dockers. On derby day in November, we were outside Anfield collecting money to support the Dockers' Fund. It was a bitterly cold day and I was holding a collection bucket, wearing a bright yellow docker's jacket and Russian-style fur hat to keep warm. Despite the strike, I had managed to remain a season ticket holder but couldn't get a ticket for the derby as it was at Anfield. Standing there, watching fans going inside was a painful experience. However, my luck changed when, from among the crowds, a fella came over to me and said, 'Ere ye are mate, I haven't got any money but here's a ticket for the match.'

I opened the ticket and it was for the Kop end. I was 26 at the time and a bit cocky so when I looked at the ticket I thought, 'I'll have a bit of that!'

I off-loaded my bucket to one of the lads collecting with me and went inside. When I got to my seat, I was to the right of the goal, seven rows from the front, although I was sat at the end of the row next to an exit. When I sat down, little did I know that my appearance there would be so well publicised.

When the two teams came out, I stood up and applauded like everyone else, so the Kopites around me didn't realise I was a Blue.

When the game started, I was quite happy as we were FA Cup holders, holding our own against the archenemy.

In the second half, a ball in from Rideout was met by Kanchelskis, whose thundering header flew in off the post past David James at the Kop end. As it entered the net, I flew out of my seat, arms flying everywhere, not realising I was so conspicuous in my luminous yellow jacket. I got a few insults and digs in the back for my celebrations but I wasn't bothered. I was by myself, deep in enemy territory, but I didn't care – my emotions just took over and I jumped everywhere.

Unbelievably, just a quarter of an hour later, the same thing happened again. This time, fantastic work by Anders Limpar played in the 'smiling assassin' Kanchelskis, who matched his earlier heroics when he cut inside a defender to crash his shot home. Once again, despite being in the 'dragon's den', alone and heavily outnumbered, my instincts got the better of me as I leapt out of my seat to celebrate our two-goal advantage. Kopites around me were obviously not too happy at my antics, especially as we were working it up them good style! Again, I took a few digs for my loyalty to the Blue cause but did not feel any pain because I was so high on emotion.

Liverpool managed to get a late consolation goal and I left with just a couple of minutes to go to in order to make a clean getaway down to County Road to meet up with my mates and toast our memorable victory.

I met up with my mates, Alec Cairns, Alan Midgley and Kevin Comer, at the County pub on the corner of Hale Road and County Road, Walton. The atmosphere, as Evertonians started pouring into the pub, was electric. The pub was bouncing as a traditional Russian tune broke out and Blues fans sang 'Andrei, Andrei Kanchelskis, da da da da da . . .'! As we were talking about the game, one of the lads I was with got on to the fact I was wearing my distinctive bright yellow jacket. He had been with the Evertonians in the Anfield Road end and had seen my luminous coat jumping up and down when we scored. When they realised it was me, news travelled round the pub and my mates, as well as a few Blues I didn't know, bought me loads of bevvies.

After many hours of drinking and singing, we moved on to the Winslow for a few more pints before going home to recapture the magic again on Match of the Day. At the end of the coverage and match interviews, Match of the Day pundit, Alan Hansen, said, 'Get on to the Kop steward behind the goal' and the cameras focused on my celebrations which even made the former handball player laugh.

Hansen, like many people, had seen me stood by an exit, wearing bright yellow and assumed I was a match steward. Because I had been highlighted on national television, I became known as 'the Kop steward'. Fanzines such as When Skies are Grey tried to find out who I was. They printed an article asking, 'Who is the Kop steward?' but I preferred to remain infamous rather than famous. Even now, more than ten years after the game, the 'Kop steward' still comes up in supporters' conversations, which makes me proud to think I was there and that was me.

Andrew still follows his beloved Blues whenever he can and remains a season ticket holder. In the future, he hopes to watch many more victories over the old enemy with his son, two-year-old Dixie.

The Derby day victory gave fans something to celebrate and what better way for a young fan to spend Christmas than following the boys of the Royle blue jersey.

Coventry City v Everton, 23 December 1995
Hitchhiker's Guide to Coventry by Jonathan Mumford

It was a couple of days before Christmas in 1995 and along with my mate Paul O'Callaghan we'd decided (without telling our parents) that we'd go to our first Everton away game. We chose Coventry because we knew it wasn't too far and we could get back in time so our parents would be none the wiser. The perfect plan.

We were 14 at the time and, despite the cold, were in good spirits and couldn't wait to get on the coach when it arrived at the Rocket pub. The driver stepped off the coach and said to us and the other two lads who were waiting with us that the coach was full and there would be another one on its way. We waited but one never arrived. We had a choice: give up and go home with our tails between our legs or hitch a lift. It was a no-brainer. I ran over to the petrol station opposite and asked the girl behind the till if I could borrow a cardboard box and a marker pen. We fashioned our very own 'Coventry' sign and took turns holding it out for passing cars. We waited for about an hour until, like some sort of messiah, a skinhead pulled up in a blue Ford Orion and told all four of us to jump in. We had nothing to lose.

His name was Phil and I'm not sure if it was the adrenalin or fear running through our young veins but everything he said was hilarious. Phil was on his way to the game too and kept us entertained with a few stories en route. What cracked us up was that after nearly every sentence he'd lift up off his seat and let rip with the loudest of farts. To a couple of naïve 14-year-old lads on a secret day out it didn't get any better. We thought he was great.

Phil walked us to the ground and arranged to meet us after the game and even offered to take us home. We couldn't believe his generosity or our good fortune. Our luck ran out at the game, however, going down 2-1 to a struggling Coventry. Noel Whelan hit the winner with a great finish but the result didn't seem that important to us. I remember Barry Horne had been dropped for the game and in protest at the end of the game he began to run laps of the pitch. We just stood there shouting him on but quickly remembered we had to meet Phil.

We half expected Phil not to be there because we did have tickets for the coach's return journey. But he was there waiting just where he said. I just remember thinking how generous he was but he just insisted he was a typical Evertonian. I didn't fully understand what it meant at the time but certainly do now.

On the way back we talked about how shit we were and Phil dropped us off at the Rocket. With smiles beaming across our faces in the knowledge that we'd succeeded in our secret mission Paul and I said our goodbyes and went our separate ways. If this was what an Everton away game was like – we wanted more.

Following the cup winners away from Goodison that season was also another young Blue – Jon Sellick.

Manchester United v Everton, 21 February 1996
VIPs by Jon Sellick

The summer of 1995 was one of the few occasions during the nineties when it was possible to be upbeat and optimistic about the Blues' prospects: Rideout's winner had capped a marvellous six months in which passionate football, an heroic centre forward and an inspiring manager had all been evident at Goodison for the first time in what seemed like an age. Now, on a wave of optimism and supported by a chairman whose ego demanded he be seen as owner-in-chief of a 'European cup winning team', it felt, for just a short while, as if we were back.

I was 14, fresh from Wembley and living in my brand new Danka top. I was with my family on the holiday of a lifetime, cruising in the Med, when I recognised a well-known face of football on board our ship. However, while he had a recognisable face, he did not have a recognisable name. I'd developed a Statto-esque football knowledge, honed from years of devouring the pages of Shoot magazine and editing my Amiga computer game, 'Sensible Soccer'. I prided myself on my footy knowledge like any fanatical 14-year-old but I still couldn't put a name to the face.

My granddad, in his 'if you don't ask, you don't get' fashion, wasted little time in introducing himself and before we knew it we were on first-name terms with Norman: Norman Davies, kit manager at Manchester United and a trusted lieutenant of Fergie. Watch any footage of United's bench in the eighties or nineties and Norman will be there. Indeed, most famously, Norman was first on hand to pull Cantona from the front row at Selhurst Park. He was also a nice fella with a warm and friendly nature, and in-depth knowledge of the football industry. Norman was a United man through and through but had nothing but kind words for the people he knew in the game with Everton connections.

Two months later, my granddad and I found ourselves in the inner sanctum of Old Trafford. It was a fantastic experience that gave us a real flavour of the workings of the club. Norman introduced us to his assistant, Albert, who took over after Norman retired. The tight-knit 'family' of Old Trafford staff we met seemed a million miles away from the Corporate Monster image portrayed by the media and I couldn't help but feel this spirit was far more integral to their success than their ability to sell a shirt in Singapore.

The big Everton news at the time was Andrei Kanchelskis. He'd finally signed for us and was about to enjoy a very successful first season at Goodison. Norman was very complimentary about the Ukrainian's personality, which boded well. Frankly, it was thrilling to get our own personal reference about a new signing from somebody who had worked with him for the previous few years. Not, however, as thrilling as being given Kanchelskis's last United shirt on the basis that they wouldn't need it again. Long-sleeved, number fourteen on the back and adorned with 'Premiership Champions' badges, it wasn't long before my seat in the Family Enclosure at Goodison allowed me to get the man himself to sign it too.

Norman told us that had it not been for Gary Pallister popping in the week before to claim Big Dunc's Cup final shirt, having swapped with him at the final whistle, he'd have given us that too. Tantalising, but any hint of disappointment was washed away by Norman's promise to get us VIP tickets for the United – Everton match that coming season.

We'd been knocked out of the cup by Port Vale the week before and were going through a wobbly patch; Kanchelskis wasn't exactly firing on all cylinders and injuries meant that Jon O'Connor made one of his few appearances. A 2-0 defeat on the night was disappointing, but I can't deny that the opportunity to follow the players down the tunnel at the final whistle more than made up for the scoreline. Norman had instructed the gateman to let us through and as Big Joe strolled past looking pretty philosophical, we hot-footed it down the tunnel and into the players' lounge.

We had the privilege of spending an hour or so in the bar and I hastily made my way round with an autograph book while my dad and granddad took snaps of me, star struck, with various players. It was the Everton players I wanted to see but there was no sign of them. Tellingly, Kanchelskis didn't make an appearance but just as I'd given up hope of seeing any Blues, in strode the stalwarts Dave Watson and Big Nev. They headed straight to their counterparts at United and spent a couple of minutes exchanging banter with Dennis Irwin, Gary Pallister and Steve Bruce. I did my best to mop up as many signatures as I could. We didn't bother with Beckham as he'd only made a few appearances, and I bottled out of asking Keane, whose aura was matched only by Cantona's. My granddad stepped on the Frenchman's foot and while he winced, thankfully, the injury didn't stop him crashing in the winner in the Cup final against Liverpool at the end of that season. Happy days!

I have the utmost respect for Everton Football Club, David Moyes and their players. That's why I love to play them, and especially at Goodison Park, where the atmosphere is magnificent.

José Mourinho, The Times, December 2006

After a slow start, the Blues made a significant improvement in the league, finishing an impressive sixth. Andrei Kanchelskis was on fire and the winger netted 13 times in the final 19 games of the season, including a hat-trick at Hillsborough..

Through the Goodison doors during the summer of 1996 came boyhood Evertonian Gary Speed, who already had a League Championship winning medal with Leeds United. The first game of the season Everton faced Newcastle Utd, winning 2-0, including a debut goal from Speed. There were even quiet murmurs of Everton mounting a title challenge, with many pundits tipping them as dark horses. After the Newcastle game Joe Royle was so impressed with Duncan Ferguson's performance that he described him as 'unplayable'.

In October, Joe Royle broke the club's transfer record for the second time, bringing in Nick Barmby from Tottenham Hotspur for £5.75m. Barmby repaid some of that money by scoring in a 7-1 mauling of Southampton. Amongst the other scorers was Gary Speed, who grabbed a hat-trick. The Blues were bang in form.

But that was to desert them during the all-important festive period and the Toffees were suddenly threatened with relegation. Things were to get even worse for Everton when, in March 1996, Joe Royle resigned. The reason thought to be behind it was the board's refusal to sanction the transfer of Norwegian striker Tore Andre Flo. Club captain Dave Watson took over as caretaker-manager and guided the Blues to safety by the narrowest of margins.

It had been expected that former Everton hero Andy Gray would take over as manager in the summer or 1997. He'd always said that the Everton job would be the only position that would see him enter football management. However, Sky, where he was employed as a pundit, made him a huge offer to stay and he turned down the Blues.

Instead, a familiar figure was to take over the reigns at Goodison Park. Howard Kendall returned for a third stint as boss. Crowd favourite Andrei Kanchelskis left for Fiorentina, Anders Limpar went to Birmingham City and FA Cup hero and journeyman Paul Rideout left for China. Everton brought in the highly rated Croatian defender Slaven Bilic for £4.5m and Gareth Farrelly from Aston Villa.

The 1997–98 season began with the same problems as the one before. The Blues managed only three wins by December. To make matters worse, Everton's greatest ever goalkeeper, Neville Southall, ended his long relationship with the club in the same month, leaving for Stoke City. Neville managed a club record 578 appearances for the Blues and is Everton's most capped player.

Four wins out of five over the Christmas period gave Evertonians some hope but before an away trip to West Ham, club skipper Gary Speed handed in a shock transfer request. He didn't play again for Everton and was snapped up by Newcastle United. A wretched run saw the Blues pick up only two wins in the remaining games of the season.

Similar to the Wimbledon game in '93, the Blues' survival hopes hinged on a last-day decider. Yet, unlike that game against 'the Crazy Gang', Everton's fate was not in their own hands. The Toffees, facing Coventry City, had to at least match Bolton Wanderers' result against Chelsea at Stamford Bridge. A very cagey game seemed to be going Everton's way when a long-range effort by Farrelly looped in and Chelsea took the lead at the Bridge. However, Barmby missed a penalty, and Dion Dublin scored at the Park End to set up a nail-biting finish. Luckily, the Blues held on and Bolton were relegated.

Howard Kendall left the club by mutual consent and, that summer, former Glasgow Rangers record-breaking manager Walter Smith took over as the new Everton boss. Smith immediately brought in new players. In came John Collins from Monaco, the combative Frenchman Olivier Dacourt and £4.5m striker Ibrahima Bakayoko.

Having spent some money bringing in some quality players there was a renewed optimism around Goodison Park. However, this optimism was to evaporate in late November. Gwladys Street's hero Duncan Ferguson was sold to Ruud Gullit's Newcastle by chairman Peter Johnson without Smith's consent. Smith was so infuriated that he threatened to resign.

Despite the unrest at Goodison Park, loyal fans continued to follow the Blues from all corners of the globe.

Arsenal v Everton, 8 November 1998
Planes, Trains and Automobiles by Ollie Williams

Like many other kids in North Wales it all began with my dad taking me by train to Liverpool. I was six and I remember nothing about the 0-0 draw against Cardiff in 1957. But I do remember the next time, a 4-0 win against a Blackpool team which included Stanley Mathews on Good Friday in 1958 in front of 65,000 fans.

A couple of visits per season became the norm for Dad and me, but I started to go more by myself in the mid 60s and in 1966 I got my first season ticket (Ground – £4.25 for 21 league games – you could stand in the Gwladys Street, Goodison Road or Park End).

My first away match was at Wolves in 1967 – I went to as many as I could afford, hitchhiking to many. I remember doing that to Carlisle in '68. I had no ticket like hundreds of others. For some reason the police and stewards stopped patrolling around the ground about 20 minutes before the end, the large gates opened up and we all piled in to see Joe Royle score Everton's second. I thought 'bunking in' was a dying art until I went to AZ Alkmaar last season where I saw an Evertonian squeeze in behind his mate in a way that Houdini would have been proud of.

Getting tickets for Cup matches was always a problem, despite having a season ticket. I failed to get one through Everton for the 1968 final (each club was allocated 16,000 tickets) but Dad got one through a connection at Wrexham FC. To this day that remains the only FA Cup final I've seen, despite seeing all those League Cup games and the Mickey Mouse cups of '89 and '91.

I left school in 1968, going to Liverpool for further study and then staying on to work for a coupe of years. I missed very few games during those years, nearly always travelling with Crown Coachways.

Those southern trips were tedious affairs – leaving Lime Street at 11:30 p.m. on a Friday night. I remember a trip to Ipswich in an old charabanc (on hire to the Crown) – engine problems and missed turnoffs meant we were late and the bus finally packed in about ten miles from Ipswich. We managed to flag down a double-decker and we filled it to the brim, meaning there was no room for the locals en route to their Saturday shopping – I hope there was a later bus.

I visited Tottenham three times in 1969–70. First we were having a pint at Euston Station when we heard heavy snow had caused a postponement. Several weeks later we went down again and the floodlights failed. The third visit was in March and ended well thanks to Alan Whittle. That occasion stands out for another reason. Liverpool put their derby match tickets on sale the same day (they sold tickets at both grounds in those days – we were allocated the entire Anfield Road end). I wrote a complaining letter to Bill Shankly, telling him that I wouldn't go anywhere near Anfield, unless Everton were playing, but I did enjoy the derby match and would be disappointed to miss it. I got a letter back.

Bill Shankly was a hate figure with Evertonians in those days but he went up in my estimation after that. A real man of the people, and his treatment by LFC after his retirement was sad. I once visited the 500 Club with Dad, and Bill was dining alone opposite us. I also said hello at Bellefield when I was on a guided tour – 'our' club became his friend and I'm glad of that.

It was in 1969 that I made my first overseas trip with the Blues – the Holyhead/Dublin ferry for the annual Shamrock Rovers friendly. In 1970–71 I went to Moenchengladbach (£26 flight, B&B, match tickets and transfers) and Panathinaikos (£39, two night's accommodation, flights and ticket).

I had the travel bug and in 1972 I travelled overland to Australia, where I remained for four years. Football news was slow to arrive; phone costs were prohibitive so it was always a rush for the Monday morning paper for the English football results. The coverage was poor in those days. There would be a highlights package once a week and only one live match a year – the Cup final. This remained the case until the early '90s when some clubs started charging £5 for a match on a Saturday night (midnight Oz time). Things are so much different now – we can even pick our match on Saturday night on our home pay TV. Last season we even had five of Everton's Euro games via Setanta.

My Kiwi partner, Lynne (we're still together) came back with me to the UK in 1976 – she wanted to see the UK and Europe. What better way than a pre-season motorbike tour to Germany for our matches in Karlsruhe, Saarbrucken and Dusseldorf, followed by fortnightly trips on the Blue Streak special to all corners of the UK? We missed three games in those two seasons – was Lynne Everton's first Kiwi season ticket holder?

We went back to Oz in 1978 after the World Cup in Argentina and set ourselves up in Sydney where we remain to this day. I got a job with an airline, which gave me access to cheap stand-by fares for annual trips to see the folks and Everton FC. That's how it was until 1993. I averaged about eight matches a season (always booked over the Easter period to maximise the number of games). The trick was to leave Oz on the Friday to arrive on the morning of a game and return after seeing a match in London.

In 1980, my flight was late into London on the Saturday morning and a later train to Middlesbrough got me there by about 2.20 p.m. – a taxi to a hotel to drop off our bags then off to the ground. We got into Ayresome Park just as the teams came on to the field.

In 1987, my return trip to Oz from Wales went via Norwich – no celebrations for me at the final whistle – just a dash for the railway station to get to Heathrow for the 10 p.m. flight to Sydney – back to work on an afternoon shift on Monday, get some overtime in and plan for Everton's post-season tour. A holiday break helped, plus several shift changes and I was off to Christchurch for the first match, then a flight to Auckland. I thought I'd have to stay two nights there, as a 3 p.m. Sunday match at the isolated MT Smart Stadium is not the easiest place from which to get a quick exit and it's a fair distance to cover to the airport for a 6.30 p.m. departure to Sydney. I approached a Maori steward outside the ground to ask where I could get a taxi after the game – problem solved. I caught the flight, and had an extra night in Sydney which gave me extra Brownie points with the Missus (on top of the ones I'd gained for visiting the in-laws).

In March 1989, I left a 90 F Sydney for Wales via St James' Park, Newcastle, for a night match where it was snowing and the Blues were abysmal.

In Oz we have a wonderful 'holiday' system at work. We accumulate 'long service leave' after ten years – three months taken as a block or in weeks as you wish. It also gives eight extra days' leave per year for additional service. I utilised this by starting to return to the UK twice a year from '93. There were lots more games for Dad and I until he died suddenly in 2000. I was made redundant in 2001; Mum had a serious illness in 2004 and so now I come home three or four times per year. I still juggle dates to maximise the number of games. I've been averaging about 25 to 30 games a season between League, Cup, friendly, youth and reserve fixtures.

Fixture alterations are a curse, but over the years, one in particular stands out. In '97 I'd booked an 'el cheapo' fare with Qantas and my return flight was 10 p.m. on Saturday night after the 3 p.m. kick-off at Highbury. On arrival in the UK, I learned the fixture had been changed to the Sunday due to Arsenal's midweek game in Eastern Europe. Due to the late change they decided to reimburse Evertonians who had pre-booked trains but there was no such generosity towards me when I told them how much it would cost to delay my flight for a day.

I turned up for the flight on the Saturday and was given a leaflet from QF saying it was 'overbooked' and would I be willing to offload and travel the following evening? If I agreed they would put me up at the Airport Hilton with meals and £200 compensation. I couldn't volunteer quickly enough and I got a £16 ticket for £20 outside High-bury the following day.

I've never managed to see every match in a season. In 1969, I caught the flu en route to Darlington for a league cup game and spent much of the match in the tea bar. My mum wouldn't let me go to Derby on the Saturday, the only match I missed that season. I've visited 70 away grounds with Everton (78 if you count new grounds). I'm one of many who've let Everton influence their lifestyle. Our home attendances and away following never ceases to amaze me – especially during the bad times, of which there have been plenty.

Walter Smith stayed on but, unfortunately for Everton, it was the same old story. The season which had started poorly never really looked like improving. Nonetheless, Everton experienced a good Cup run in 1999, making it to the quarter-final stages. Their first opponents in the third round were Bristol City, and the Blues made the long trip to Ashton Gate. With performances below expectations, fans were drowning their sorrows even before kick-off.

FA Cup 3rd Round, Bristol City v Everton, 2 January 1999
Two Triple Whiskies Please by Jonathan Mumford

Still nursing one of those 48-hour hangovers from New Year's Eve, I wasn't looking forward to the drive to Bristol. As I was the only one with a car (we were all poor students at the time) I was the designated driver. I remember picking up my mates, Dougie, Ocky and Dougie's mate, Silker, from their houses and setting off southwards. I didn't know Silker but I'd heard stories that he was a bit of a nutter. The drive down was fine – the traffic wasn't too bad and the hangover was subsiding.

We parked up and followed the sea of blue that was heading for the local ale house. Silker headed straight to the bar and ordered two triple whiskies. After a few more large Jack Daniel's we headed into the ground. As always, our support was fantastic that day – we filled the end behind one goal at Ashton Gate and we were in good voice.

The game itself was rubbish and we were being outplayed by a team two divisions below us. During this period we had Danny Cadamarteri and £4.5m signing Ibrahima Bakayoko up front. After a very slow start, Bakayoko had found the net a few times leading up to the game and held all our hopes.

As I said, the game was poor, and it wasn't until the last five minutes that we had our first real chance. It was a free kick about 30 yards out and Bakayoko and Don Hutchison stood over it. Bakayoko just lashed it into the top corner and the Evertonians went mad. A minute later the win was wrapped up with Bakayoko's second. As I was hugging my mates in celebration I noticed one of our party was missing. It was Dougie's mate Silker.

The game finished and we waited around for him but he was nowhere to be found. This was before anyone had a mobile phone so we couldn't ring him or send a quick text so we just waited. And waited. We came to the conclusion that in his pissed state he had either gone back to the pub or was waiting at my car. We made our way back to the car, still in awe of Bakayoko's thunderbolt, but occasionally remembering our lost friend. No sign in the pub. Nor at the car. We waited again – this time for about an hour. There was nothing else we could do so we set off home. We got home really late but had Match of the Day taped and put it on to see our victory. A bit sleepy-eyed, I watched as Bakayoko stroked in his second. In the background I saw a few Evertonians on the pitch. And there he was in all his drunken glory, a drunken Silker trying to hug Everton's new hero. It all made sense. Dougie spoke to him the next day and was told by Silker that the police were not best pleased by his unexpected appearance. As he tried to run back off the pitch he was arrested and spent the night in Bristol prison along with a good few others. It was a great day out and it always makes me laugh when I think about Silker's antics.

Without the goalscoring of the on-loan Kevin Campbell, who netted nine times in the final six games of the season, the Blues would certainly have been relegated. As it was, they finished 14th in the Premiership. Such was Everton's poor form in the 1998–99 season that one important fan proved you could barely give away a ticket to watch the Blues.

Everton Football Club currently has approximately 900 stockholders, of whom just over 150 are members of the Shareholders Association. Paul Wharton is an integral member. Here he remembers a trip to Old Trafford.

Manchester Utd v Everton, 21 March 1999
Spares for the Mayors by Paul Wharton

It's not often that football gets the publicity that it deserves. The media always like to publish the harsher side of life. Hopefully this story will give a little balance to the good side of football.

As I set off to the Man Utd away game in March 1999 with a spare ticket for the match in my pocket I thought it would be easy to get rid of it before the game. How wrong can you be? My mate had let me down at the last minute and not wanting to waste a trip to Old Trafford, I decided to get rid of it on the day. After all, it was two of the biggest clubs facing each other in front of 55,000 fans. I didn't really fancy hanging around but with about two minutes to go there were still no takers. In desperation, I approached an older man who, with bucket in hand, was collecting for charity. I approached him, asking, 'Are you not going to the game today?' In a Manchester accent he replied that he wasn't.

'No Ticket.'

Perfect. 'Here's a ticket,' I said, handing it over.

He looked at it and said, 'So I will have to be an Evertonian today then, will I? OK, no problem. How much do you want for it?'

I told him he could have the ticket for free as I had been let down and I knew the game was about to kick off. We wished each other well and I shouted 'Enjoy the match' as I made my way into the stadium.

The game itself was predictable. Despite holding our own in the first 45 minutes, United's class told in the second half with three goals in 15 minutes to put the result beyond doubt. Don Hutchison scored a free kick to salvage some pride but we went away empty-handed.

I found out later that the man who took my ticket had attempted to make contact via the letters page of the Liverpool Echo. However, I didn't buy the paper that week. A few weeks later my good friend, David Vickers, rang after reading the Newcastle Utd home programme. He informed me that the man I gave the ticket to at Old Trafford was looking for me and had advertised in the programme.

'Do you know who he is?' David asked.

'I've no idea,' I replied.

'His name is Harry Faulkner, and he's the Deputy Mayor of the borough of Trafford!'

When I found this out I telephoned Harry. He thanked me again and told me that the following year he would be Mayor of Trafford. 'When you visit Old Trafford with Everton FC next season, I would like you to be my special guest,' he said.

I was flabbergasted, to say the least. I went to the game and sat next to a Man Utd legend in the front row of the directors' box. Bill Foulkes was one of the few Busby Babes to survive the Munich air crash and was made club captain after the disaster. Again, the Blues were on the receiving end of a defeat; a rather more convincing 5-1 loss. Despite taking an early lead through Franny Jeffers, Everton were never in it. Man Utd cruised to a victory which included four goals from Ole Gunnar Solskjaer.

The fact that I was sitting in the directors' box made the defeat slightly easier to take but it also made me realise the generosity that exists between football fans that often goes unnoticed. And it just goes to show you never know who you are talking to.

Over the next two or three seasons Everton remained in the bottom half of the Premiership. The future looked very bleak. Then again, we could still dream . . .

The 2000s

Everton v Tottenham Hotspur,
13 January 2001
Spencer Collects the Trophy for Everton by Barry Spencer

'. . . and Spencer collects the Cup for Everton.'

Then I woke up. Many a school hour was happily spent daydreaming of collecting silverware for Everton. Sometimes at Wembley, sometimes in Europe, beating Liverpool, Ajax or Bayern Munich, often by 4-3 having been 3-0 down with five minutes left to play. Ball, Kendall and Harvey would take control of the midfield. Three quick goals would level the score (the goal scorers varied but I had a hand in all of them). Bally would then thread the ball through to me on the wing. Beating four men I would cross the ball with pinpoint accuracy for Joe Royle to head home, or he'd nod it down to me to volley home if I was on a hat-trick.

Despite Brian Labone's offer to let me pick up the trophy, I'd point out that he was the captain and I was quite content just to pick up the man-of-the-match award.

They say if you wish for something hard enough . . .

By the time I reached thirty, I began to come to terms with the fact that it was unlikely an Everton talent scout would spot me and that I wouldn't be collecting silverware for Everton. But on 13 January 2001 the call came from Everton.

Alan Myers, the club's PR man, was organising a parade of the players who'd won the Championship in 1970 as part of the launch of the Players' Foundation and had the idea of having the trophy there for the champions to hold once more. The only problem was that it was at The Valley, home of Charlton Athletic, as the trophy is still presented to the First Division champions.

John Collings, the travel co-ordinator for the Everton Supporters' Club London Area (ESCLA), had told Alan that I lived not too far from The Valley. When Alan asked if I would pick it up I was only too happy to oblige. I considered it a great honour to be helping Everton and what's more it was nice to help Alan in particular as he has often gone out of his way to help ESCLA.

So I got the train from work to Charlton and collected the trophy after showing a fax from the Football League giving me permission to take it. It comes in a wooden box with League Championship Trophy printed using a Dyno label maker. Real class! I got a cab home (the thought of leaving it on the bus was too scary to contemplate) and once safely there I placed it on top of the telly where it resided for the evening while I gazed lovingly at it during the advert breaks in Buffy the Vampire Slayer and Angel.

My mate Joe Williams (a Charlton fan) came round and we took a few pictures but I had to decline his offer of a drink as I couldn't leave the trophy unguarded. (I could have taken it down the pub with me, but after a few drinks I might have lost it in a card game).

The following day I took it to Euston by cab. As we went past the police barriers in the City the cabbie pointed out that if the police searched the cab we'd be spending the afternoon in a cell!

Once we got to Euston, I met up with my Tottenham mate Fred Dowry (who surprisingly recognised the trophy). Any ESCLA member around was accosted with the words, 'You'll never guess what I've got in this box.' After being caressed by many Blues, and kissed by Paul

McMonnies, the trophy was passed on to John Collings who took it on the coach. I was in a group travelling by train and we considered it prudent the trophy should go by coach because the train might be delayed.

JC took it to the ground and, following the appearance of West, Brown, Kendall, Husband, Whittle, Kenyon and Jackson, Brian Labone proudly brought the trophy on to the pitch. Unfortunately my two biggest heroes, Joe Royle and Alan Ball, couldn't be there. But the other teammates of my fantasies from thirty years before were there looking as proud as I was. After all, we'd all achieved the honour of bringing the trophy home to Goodison.

Soon after, Bill Kenwright's consortium managed to take control of the club once he had bought out Peter Johnson. On the playing side, the Goodison faithful were delighted when Duncan Ferguson re-signed for £3.75m. They were, however, horrified when Nick Barmby did the unthinkable and moved across Stanley Park in a £6m deal. Also brought in were a number of older players who had frankly seen better days.

The general view around this period was that Everton played too defensively. To combat this perception, players such as Paul Gascgoine, David Ginola and Mark Hughes were signed as short-term fixes to larger problems. None of them were a real success and it was inevitable that Walter Smith left the club in March 2002.

Bill Kenwright turned to David Moyes on 14 March 2002. A very young but talented manager, he endeared himself to the Blues fans at his first press conference. Moyes decribed Everton as 'The People's Club', referring to the fact that the people on the street support Everton and it is very much a club with loyal fans. The quote really struck a chord with Evertonians; so much so that it has been adopted by the club as their slogan.

Moyes' first game was a home fixture against Fulham. David Unsworth got the new manager off to the perfect start, drilling a left-foot strike into the bottom corner of the net within a minute of the kick-off. Moyes eventually steadied the ship and guided the Blues to 15th place.

David Moyes' first full season at Everton was always when he would be judged. To help the cause he brought in Joseph Yobo from Marseille and had an immediate clear-out of older players such as Ginola and Jesper Blomqvist.

The Blues made an excellent start, even placing themselves in the top three at one stage. There was definitely more emphasis on youth with Moyes at the helm. The finest example was when he gave a debut to a certain Wayne Rooney in October 2002 at the tender age of 16. Rooney scored one of the goals of the season in the last minute to secure a win over title contenders Arsenal.

A series of 1-0 victories ensured that the Blues maintained their standards towards the end of the season. However, they slipped eventually to seventh, being pipped to a European place by Blackburn Rovers on the final day. Such an impressive debut season for such a young and inexperienced manager justifiably earned David Moyes the Manager of the Year award.

With their team making excellent progress under Moyes' stewardship the previous season, Evertonians were optimistic that the team would push on and build on the progress made. However, frustrated by some failed purchases, Moyes was under pressure to sign players due to the new transfer window system. On the final day of business, he signed four players including James McFadden and Nigel Martyn. The latter, Moyes was to say years later, was his best ever signing.

A very poor run of form from January saw Everton scrapping around at the wrong end of the table. It seemed as though it was business as usual and Everton were back on a downward slide. A 17th place finish, one place above the relegation zone, and a points total of just 39 meant that Everton had endured another very disappointing season.

Bill Kenwright stood by Moyes at the end of this miserable season when it would have been easier to replace him. His loyalty paid off in a big way in 2003–04.

Evertonians began the season with a very pessimistic mindset the following year. This was due to the sale of 'wonderkid' Wayne Rooney to Manchester United for £30m. Rooney, who once revealed a T-shirt displaying the words 'Once a Blue, always a Blue' in response to media speculation regarding his future, quickly went from hero to villain. To compensate for the loss of Rooney, Moyes brought in Tim Cahill from Millwall for £2.5m as well as journeyman Marcus Bent.

The sale of Rooney somehow seemed to galvanise the team. Now without any real 'stars', the team placed huge importance on teamwork and togetherness. One highlight and a perfect example of this team spirit was Lee Carsley's winner in the Goodison derby and the ensuing 'piley on' by the whole team. Everton broke their transfer record to sign James Beattie from Southampton in a £6m deal but Beattie's first season never really got going due to injury and suspension.

Thomas Gravesen was in fine form during the first part of the season; so much so that he was snapped up by Real Madrid in the January transfer window. To take his place as the craftsman of the team was the on-loan Mikel Arteta, a skilful young Spaniard.

The Blues held a top-four place for the majority of the season and miraculously managed to hold off their rivals Liverpool for the coveted fourth Champions League place. In the process they became the first team to threaten the dominance of the so-called 'Big Four'. As a result of the feat (having managed to finish fourth on a shoestring) Moyes was again named Manager of the Year.

Everton were into the qualifying stages of the Champions League in 2005–06 and expectations were high. Moyes brought in Phil Neville to provide some much-needed experience, Simon Davies and full-back Nuno Valente, a Champions League winner with Porto. While these signings didn't have the Evertonians salivating, they still had an excellent chance of progressing to the Champions League group stages – a real money spinner.

But Evertonians will remember the disallowed goal which cost them a place in the Champions League proper. Pierluigi Colina, the most respected referee in the game, adjudged Duncan Ferguson to have fouled a Villarreal defender while heading into the net. Replays proved the decision to be very harsh. The Blues were then automatically entered into the UEFA Cup and, still sporting a hangover from their Champions League exploits, were embarrassed against Dinamo Bucharest, completely capitulating and losing 5-2 on aggregate.

These results meant Everton had squandered an excellent opportunity to build on their impressive league achievements and their poor form continued into the Premiership. In the first eight games of the 2005–06 season, Everton managed to win only one game. Despite this setback, loyal Evertonians were still singing.

West Bromwich Albion v Everton, 19 November 2005
Smigger, the 'Rough' Diamond by Harry Shandy

In the 1980s I was living in Somerset and due to get married to a girl from the area. Before the wedding we were invited to Liverpool to meet some of her family as her dad was from Kirkby. I somehow imagined that Kirkby was a small quiet village so was a bit surprised when we arrived at a house opposite the old Kirkby Town football club.

The family had put on a party for us and, as usually happens at house parties, the men congregated in the kitchen while the women stayed out of the way in the living room.

In the kitchen, naturally the topic of conversation was football and one of the men asked which team I followed. I told him it was the most successful British team ever – Linfield from my home city of Belfast. When they heard that, they started to waffle on a load of crap about Liverpool's history and gave me stick about supporting Linfield. I was only young at the time and the more they went on, the more the hairs stood up on the back of my neck. After I'd takein a load of stick, one of them asked me which team I supported in England. I knew Everton were a team from Liverpool as well, so, to get my own back and wind them up, I told them I supported Everton. They took the bait and I was able to get some of my own back and wind them up for a change by saying how much I loved Everton.

After the party, we returned to Somerset and, during the week, my girlfriend said 'I've got you a ticket for Saturday.'

'A ticket for what?' I said.

'A ticket to go and watch Everton.'

'But I don't support Everton. What made you think that?'

'At the party I heard you talking about Everton when you were in the kitchen; saying how much you loved them.'

Thinking I was a keen Everton supporter she had got me a ticket for the following match and also organised travel from Somerset to Liverpool with two Everton fans from her village, one a local, the other a Scouser.

I can't remember who Everton played that day but as soon as I went to Goodison Park, that was it, I was hooked. Details of the game may have long gone from my memory but I'll never forget the fans' humour that day. They were so funny and quick-witted. I enjoyed myself so much that I travelled more than 400 miles to and from every home game after that and never missed a game.

Eventually I couldn't settle in Somerset so decided to go to Liverpool as I felt it was the closest thing to being back home in Belfast.

I continued watching Everton and became friends with many fans. Over the years we travelled away to watch the Blues and had some great laughs. On one occasion we went on a minibus to West Brom. Even after being beaten 4-0, the humour was good and despite the scoreline we still enjoyed the game. On the way home we decided to go for a drink to drown our sorrows. We pulled off the M6 just after Birmingham and drove down around two to three miles of country lanes until we reached a village pub.

The pub was heaving. The locals resembled something out of Royston Vasey with black trousers and white socks. Everyone looked very similar, which, coupled with the dress sense, indicated a small gene pool.

Around ten of us were stood at the bar having a pint when we noticed a DJ had karaoke equipment. One of the lads, Paul Smith, thinks he's a Neil Diamond sound-alike although in truth he murders any number he sings. On seeing the DJ, a few of the lads, knowing how bad he is, started to wind him up saying 'Go on Smigger, get up there!'

Before we knew it, he was talking to the DJ with microphone in hand. As the background music began to play, he turned to the audience and, in true cabaret style, said, 'Good evening, ladies and gentlemen, my name's Smigger from Old Swan in Liverpool and I'm gonna sing a song for you.'

At this point we turned away, knowing that they were about to hear the worst possible rendition of 'Hello Again'. Not shy coming forward, Smigger, thinking he's the bee's knees, moved towards all the old dears sat on the front row. Crooning away as if he was Tom Jones, he started touching their hands and they began to go weak at the knees in admiration – or possibly disbelief. You could see the fags in the hands of the old girls shaking as Smigger edged closer towards them. Normally he gets booed off wherever he goes but after this performance, the audience rose to give him a standing ovation.

After milking the applause and resisting encores, we decided to leave. As we were going, one of the locals asked 'Will you be coming back next year?'

After our 4-0 drubbing, still maintaining a sense of humour, we said 'We mightn't be in the Premiership next year!'

During the journey back, Smigger wouldn't shut up about his performance and still asks to go back there as that's the only place in the country that's ever liked him.

In many ways this story shows just how unique Everton supporters are. Even in adversity, we maintain our humour, which prevents us becoming disillusioned. Our loyalty knows no bounds yet we are deeply realistic. For us, Everton is a way of life. Even without success for many years we still have a large fan base, particularly away from home where we regularly fill our allocation. There has to be something special for you to do that week in, week out, especially without seeing something special on the pitch, which we haven't seen for a long time. For me, being an Evertonian is everything. It's a way of life for me now.

These defeats seemed to knock the wind out of Everton's sails and the Toffees finished 11th in the Premier League. However, one Blues supporter had an experience in London not to be forgotten.

West Ham v Everton, 4 March 2006
King for a Day by Ian Simpson

I was invited down to West Ham by a couple of mates of mine from the East End of London who were big Hammers fans and, as it was a corporate job, and a freebie, I accepted.

We were picked up from our hotel in Huntingdon in a limousine and arrived at Upton Park around 12 o'clock. As we were in corporate hospitality, all of us were suited and booted but the hospitality boxes weren't ready to take us at this time, so one of the West Ham fans called Wolfie suggested we went for a quick pint until it was time to go in.

The pub he selected was called The Boleyn, situated just round the corner from Upton Park. It was a pub with a bit of a reputation and had been used as a setting in the film Green Street, which told the story of football hooligans from West Ham's infamous 'ICF'. As I was the only Evertonian and Scouser in the gang, Wolfie said before we entered, 'Simo, keep yer mairf shat! It can get a bit tasty in here.'

As soon as you went in there was a proud notice saying that it had been used in the film, and it was easy to see why such a location had been chosen. I glanced round and saw skinheads covered in tattoos with cauliflower ears and broken noses – and they were just the barmaids!

The cockneys I was with, Wolfie and Robbo, knew a lot of the motley crew in there so after a few minutes I started to relax and enjoy a few pints until nature started to take its course and I had to go and splash the boots. As I was at the urinal a big skinhead around 6ft 4ins came in, stood next to me and said 'Awright mate?' Remembering Wolfie's advice about remaining tight-lipped I slowly glanced up to acknowledge him and, in my best Jim Davidson voice said 'Awright' before exiting sharpish. When I got back to the lads I was with and told them they laughed their heads off.

Fortunately by now it was time to go to the ground so we made our way to the executive lounge at Upton Park. My first impression of West Ham's ground was that it reminded me a bit of Goodison Park as it has a church situated at the ground and the streets outside were similar to County Road, Walton. Inside, though, it has a hotel, the rooms of which on match days are altered and used for corporate hospitality. At the end of the game, boxes become rooms again.

In corporate hospitality you are greeted by table walkers. These are usually former players who act as ambassadors for the club by talking to fans before and after the game. Ours was Frank McAvennie, who played for The Hammers in the 1980s, forming a potent strike partnership with our very own Tony Cottee. Frank knew the lads I was with and they called him over to our table. In his heyday Frank was a Scottish international, a player in the mould of Arsenal's Charlie Nicholas, a champagne Charlie who loved the birds and the booze.

When he came over it was apparent he had not been home for a while. Despite being dressed in a suit, he looked like a tramp. He explained to us that he hadn't been home for four days and that he lived somewhere in the north-east because his wife wouldn't let him live in either Scotland or London because when he's in those places he just goes missing on benders for days at a time. As he sat down it was clear that he was still pissed and a bit the worse for wear. One of the lads asked if he wanted a drink, to which he replied, 'Aye, I'll have a large vodka and coke.'

During the match he visited our table regularly and in between more large vodka and cokes, we got talking about matches he'd played against Everton over the years. Frank was very complimentary about Everton and its supporters, likening us in many ways to West Ham, particularly regarding our genuineness and loyalty.

While Frank was staggering from table to table down our end, working the tables at the opposite end of the ground was Tony Cottee. Robbo knew Tony personally so, after the final whistle, he rang him on his mobile. 'Alright TC, it's Robbo, where are you?' he said. Tony Cottee said he was on the opposite side by the hotel block. 'I've got a mate here who's an Evertonian who wants to meet you.'

Cottee said, 'Yeah, no worries, bring him across.'

Off we went. Tony Cottee had given Robbo his room number so we walked around until we came to one of the executive boxes with pitchside views that after the game become hotel rooms.

Robbo said, 'I think this is it here' as we stopped outside a room with a closed door. By this time we were bladdered and instead of knocking first, Robbo just barged straight in followed closely by me. To our surprise, instead of being greeted by Everton's former goalscoring hero, we were actually encountered by a fella having a bit of 'how's your father' on a bed with two dolly birds. Robbo and I stood there in amazement, but the fella just smiled – as you would in his position!

Robbo said 'OK mate?' before the two of us made a quick U-turn and left. I wondered how much he might have paid for this special corporate hospitality but decided against going back to ask him as he looked busy.

Tony Cottee was next door and he, in stark contrast to Frank McAvennie, looked fit, although not as fit as the two stunners we had interrupted moments earlier. Before I'd met him, I'd heard a few things about Tony Cottee but, like McAvennie, he was also very complimentary about Everton, especially its supporters, who gave him great backing during his time at Goodison. TC signed a couple of programmes I had with me and then asked what we were doing later. Robbo told him we had a table booked at Peter Stringfellow's nightclub in the West End.

'Do me a favour,' said TC. 'Don't tell Frank. He'll want to go with you and we're supposed to be doing some after-dinner speaking later. If he hears you're off there he won't show.'

We said we wouldn't and left TC to make our way over to the Players' Lounge.

At around 7.30 p.m. we arrived at Stringfellow's for our meal. We were seated by several scantily dressed hostesses who also offer extra services such as head massage. Wolfie was up for some of what was available and got his head massaged by a tasty little Thai bird for £25. His lad was also with us and as she was rubbing Wolfie's baldy head he shouted to his son 'Don't tell your mavva.' As you could get a lap dance in Liverpool for a fiver. I declined some generous offers, choosing instead to watch the lads enjoying theirs.

At the end of our table was a leopardskin throne used by Peter Stringfellow when he is in his club. After our meal, Wolfie shouted to one of the hostesses and asked her if Peter was coming in that night. When she said no, he leapt into it and I followed him soon afterwards. There I was, king for a day and what a day it had been. The only way it would have been better is if Everton would have won instead of drawing the game 2-2.

The 2006–07 season began with renewed optimism and the club once again had one eye on the allimportant Champions League. David Moyes broke the club transfer record for a second successive year with the £8.6m acquisition of Andrew Johnson from newly relegated Crystal Palace and the prospect of him and James Beattie up front had Evertonians positively purring. The Championship was again Moyes' place of business when snapping up Joleon Lescott from Wolves. Lescott had been coveted by many Premier League clubs but none were prepared to take the gamble due to a chequered past regarding injuries. US goalkeeper Tim Howard arrived on a loan deal which eventually became permanent the following year. All three added some muchneeded quality in key areas of the park.

Johnson's blistering pace and high work rate, Lescott's tidy defending and Howard's consistent reliability ensured the Blues' league form flourished again. One of the highlights for Evertonians was the 3-0 drubbing of Liverpool at Goodison Park in which Johnson immediately endeared himself to the Gwladys Street. Most Evertonians will remember the atmosphere in the stadium that day, capped off wonderfully by Pepe Reina, Liverpool's keeper, dropping a howler in front of the Park End and Johnson gratefully accepting his gift to complete his brace and the 3-0 win. The image of Goodison's new hero gesturing the 3-0 scoreline to the home fans after Reina's error is one that will live long in the memory.

In the cups, Everton did not enjoy as much success. The Blues were defeated in the League Cup by Arsène Wenger's young Arsenal side at Goodison, unlucky to go down 1-0. Despite the blistering start made by Johnson, his goalscoring touch evaded him in the next few months but such was Everton's quality that the goals were shared right through the team. A fantastic game at home to Chelsea broke Everton hearts. Having led 2-1 through Beattie and Yobo, the Blues allowed Lampard the space to equalise. Seconds from the end Didier Drogba scored a thunderbolt of a volley and Everton were left pointless.

Moyes' wretched record in the FA Cup was to continue with a 4-1 defeat at home to Blackburn Rovers in the third round. Later that month the Goodison crowd were going Rocky crazy. Sylvester Stallone, Everton's newest fan, was a guest of Bill Kenwright for a match against Reading in a shrewd ploy both to promote his new film Rocky Balboa and help raise the Blues' profile. Stallone even attended his premiere in London with the famous royal blue scarf around his neck.

An injury to key midfielder Tim Cahill meant Everton's push for the Champions League lost momentum and the Blues eventually secured sixth and UEFA Cup football for the following season. Everton's player of the year was rightly Mikel Arteta, the gifted Spaniard entertaining Evertonians with his deft skill and deadball specialism.

It was in the 2007–08 season that Everton cemented themselves as consistent challengers to the top four, finally ending the cycle of alternating between the top and bottom halves of the league. As Moyes entered his sixth season at the helm Everton were again the team asking all the questions of the Big Four. During this season Moyes brought in three invaluable players to Everton. The transfer record was again smashed to secure the services of Yakubu for £11.25m. Steven Pienaar came on loan and Phil Jagielka was brought in from Sheffield United for £4m.

In order to progress to the group stages of the UEFA Cup, the Blues had to overcome a tricky tie against the relatively unknown Metalist Kharkiv of the Ukraine. Two Evertonians made the trip and very nearly stayed a lot longer than anticipated.

Metalist Kharkiv v Everton, 4 October 2007
Captain Scarlet by Alec Cairns

It was a funny old trip. We actually got the last two places on the official Everton trip to see the Blues take on Metalist in the UEFA Cup. We had decided to go as we had disappointingly drawn the first leg at Goodison and thought we might not get another European tour with the Blues for years. We made arrangements to meet up with the rest of the boys, who had decided to travel down from Kiev.

Before we went, I decided to prepare properly and checked the world weather forecast. I saw that the weather looked good out there – about 70 degrees – so dressed appropriately. We arrived at the airport first thing in the morning and everyone was dressed in big parka jackets with woolly hats because of the reputation for cold weather out there. We just stood there in our shorts and T-shirts and were interviewed by Radio City. But that was before it all kicked off.

Deciding against staying over in Kharkiv, we agreed to go straight in, watch the match and then come straight out. It was pretty much a normal flight on our way out despite the fact that there was no ale allowed on board. But we knew we'd make up for that when we got to Kharkiv. When we arrived, there were about five coachloads of fans and on each coach was a Thomson rep in charge of that party.

The girl allocated to our coach told us that it was her first job. Ever. She took all our names and tickets and we set off into the town centre. Before leaving the airport we were dying for a drink but it looked like some sort of military airbase with no shops. There was one vending machine that sold ale so we bought every can and made our way to the coach. Our rep told us there was no ale allowed on the coach but we took it on anyway.

We met up with all the other Blues in the main square at about 3 o'clock (seven hours before kick-off) and that's when it properly started. There were these booths over there that sold ciggies and sweets and stuff but they also sold big litre bottles of Beck's for 30p. We filled our boots and then went to some bars, going straight on the 'wodka' shots and deciding to have vodka races with these Ukrainians we met. The Ukrainians were absolutely made up with all the Everton fans and seemed to be having a great time, even asking for photos. There must have been about 2,500 Everton fans in this square and there was a real party atmosphere.

We got to the ground and somehow we lost each other. Alan had my ticket and I couldn't find him anywhere. He told me later on that he was ringing me and waiting outside the gates. He didn't know that I was already in there. I still don't know to this day how I got in with-out a ticket – one minute I was waiting outside looking for Alan, the next I'm in the ground with everyone. The atmosphere was great, but when we went 2-1 down Alan just said to me 'I've had enough – I'm going – I'm going for another wodka.' So he left and went to a bar. Later on he told me he heard a shout as he was leaving and presumed the final score was 2-2. So off he went to a bar that was apparently full of Ukrainians and had some wodka shots with them.

After the game I went looking for him and there was a little bit of trouble outside the ground. Due to the fact that we didn't know anything of the law out there I knew I needed to steer clear. Luckily, we found each other and I knew we needed to head straight back to the coach as time was getting on. Alan told me about the bar he was in and the next thing I knew we were walking away from the coaches and back into a bar. I was telling Alan that the coach was leaving soon but Alan wouldn't listen – he told me to come and meet his new Ukrainian mates. We got two pints of ale each and I then realised we really had better get going because we were going to miss the coach. Before we left Alan gave his Everton top to a Ukrainian and received only a scarf in return, which he draped over his bare shoulders.

We walked out of the bar, still with our ale in each hand, to where the coaches were and it was deserted. Not a soul there. The ground was in the middle of a huge industrial estate so we didn't know what to do or where to walk to get a taxi. The next thing, this old Skoda screeches up next to us and these Ukrainian grocks get out who are dressed like they're in the military – looking like Captain Scarlet with guns in holsters – the lot. And we're just standing there with our ale and Alan's just got this scarf on.

We said 'Airport, airport.' They took the pints off us and threw them on the floor. They then pointed to the car as if to say 'Get in that car.' We were just thinking 'What the f*** is going on here?'

When we got in the car there was an oldish fella sitting in the back and I was like 'All right mate – are you an Everton fan like us?' but he just looked at me blankly. I then put my arm on the shoulder rest on the seat in front to talk to Alan and this old fella slapped it down as if it was an impolite gesture.

At this point I'd sobered up a bit, realising the seriousness of the situation. There was no such luck with Alan. He turned to me and said 'I can't believe we drew 2-2,' to which I replied 'We won.'

With that Alan started singing and shouting and ruffling the hats on these military types and even started honking their noses. Added to this we were driving through Kharkiv and we're doing about 100 miles an hour through the streets, still with no idea where they were taking us. I was convinced we were going to jail and just thought 'What's gonna happen to me in a Ukrainian jail – and I'm the handsome one!'

Eventually we pulled up to this deserted place in this Skoda and as we got out there was a huge line of heavily armed military officers. It didn't look good – I just remember thinking that we could be locked up for ages. We were then led forwards and we realised it was the airport and we were the first ones back!

When our coach turned up, the rep was there crying her eyes out thinking she'd lost two passengers on her very first job and we said 'We're here!'

The flight home was less dramatic and we were so drained, both physically and emotionally, that we conked out for the whole five hours, waking up at John Lennon Airport. The next day Alan rang me and was chatting as if nothing had happened. He couldn't remember a thing about it so I had to tell him the story of how we nearly got locked up in a Ukrainian military prison, and that it was all his fault!

Everton ultimately missed out on fourth but secured fifth, their second successive top six finish. Moyes' knockout results improved massively. Everton reached the semi-final of the Carling Cup and having conceded a very important late goal in the first leg lost out narrowly at Goodison to Chelsea.

There was more heartbreak in the UEFA Cup. Sandwiched in between excellent home wins against Zenit St Petersburg and Larissa (which must include a mention for a magical goal by Leon Osman) was the tricky away trip to Nuremberg. For some fans even the seemingly straightforward trip to Germany was a lot trickier than they could ever have anticipated.

Nuremberg v Everton, UEFA Cup group stage, 8 November 2007
And If You Know Your Geography, by Terry Padden

It was great to be back in Europe again and finally make the group stages of the UEFA Cup. You never know how far Everton will go in Europe, or when they'll be back, so you have to make the most of every opportunity that comes along. Thousands of Evertonians saw the relatively short journey to Nuremberg, Germany, as one such opportunity. They included me and my mates, Ste Duffy and Paul Herd.

On the internet I found a London tour company offering a two-day trip to Germany for £299 so gave them a call. The fella I spoke to described what sounded like a good deal – a flight from Liverpool to Stuttgart with a half-hour stopover, then on to Nuremberg to spend two nights in a city centre, four-star hotel. Taking him at his word I booked for the three of us and the tickets arrived a few days later.

I put them to one side and opened the envelope three days before we were due to leave. When I checked the details I was upstairs, while the girl I was living with at the time was downstairs. Suddenly, she heard me screaming and rushed upstairs to see what was wrong. When she found me, I was waving the tickets, screaming 'Palma! Palma Nova!'

Instead of travelling directly to Germany, we had been put on to a flight to Palma Nova which included a six-hour stay in Majorca that would make our flying time approximately 14 hours!

After my bird eventually calmed me down, I rang the other lads to inform them of our new itinerary. When I told them we were going to Germany via Majorca, their reaction was 'What are we doing going there?' Imagine their surprise then, when I told them we would be coming back via Budapest, Hungary!

On Wednesday, 7 November I got up around half-past four in the morning and made my way to Speke airport. We left Liverpool and got to Palma Nova at 9.00 a.m., bracing ourselves for our six-hour wait. The weather at the airport was roasting hot. Holidaymakers dressed in T-shirts and shorts looked at us, sweating in our winter coats, as if to say 'What are you doing here?'

With six hours to kill, our only option was to take off our parkas and go ouy on to the terrace to catch a few rays.

We boarded our plane to Nuremberg at 3.30 p.m. and took our seats along with 200 German tourists going home from their holidays. Once again we got funny looks, including from the trolley dolly who stared at us before asking 'What are you doing here?'

Eventually we arrived in Nuremberg at 8.30 p.m., some fifteen hours after leaving Liverpool. However, once again our plans were dealt another blow when we discovered that our hotel wasn't even in Nuremberg. Instead, it was about an hour outside the city, so far away that the taxi driver didn't even know where it was.

The following day we made our way into Nuremberg and spent the day with the six or seven thousand Blues fans. I'd been abroad to watch Everton play in European competitions and pre-season friendlies but the atmosphere that day was the best ever.

We got on sound with the Nuremberg fans and the German people and the 2-0 victory capped off a memorable night as Evertonians celebrated well into the early hours. We drank along with them of course, but the only downer for us was the thought of a one-hour, £40 taxi ride to our hotel and an early rise the following day to catch our flight to Budapest.

On day three of the tour we woke early, made our way to the airport and boarded our flight to Hungary.

At 11.30 a.m. we landed in Budapest's Ferihegy International Airport where we were faced with a nineandahalfhour wait for our connection to Liverpool. We sat there counting down the hours. I sat, for around eight hours, just staring at the TV monitors showing the outbound flight information. I kept saying to myself 'It'll be up in a minute, it'll be up in a minute' but nothing happened.

Our intended departure time was edging nearer and nearer so I said to the lads, 'I'll have to sort this out' and went over to ask what was going on. I enquired about our flight only to be told we were at the wrong airport terminal!

We didn't know, but there is more than one airport terminal at Budapest airport and, sod's law, we were at the wrong one. When we realised, we ran outside and over to a bus parked near to the terminal. Unfortunately, the bus driver couldn't understand three desperate Scousers trying to explain they were at the wrong airport terminal and needed to be at the other one in less than half an hour. Thankfully, a woman on the bus spoke English and she interpreted for us. The bus took around fifteen minutes to reach the other terminal and we boarded our flight with about five minutes to spare. God knows what would have happened if that woman hadn't been there to help us – we'd probably still be there now.

There were no pre-booked seats on this flight so people made a dash for the best seats as soon as they got on. The three of us made our way straight to the front of the plane and sat down in the chairs with the extra legroom. Women, children and the fifty or so Hungarian Kopites on board looked on at us but we said, 'We're staying here and if you knew what we'd been through, you'd understand.'

We slept all the way home and finally made it back to Liverpool after travelling more than thirty hours to a place that took most fans about three hours. When I told my dad what had happened he contacted Roger Phillips on BBC Radio Merseyside as well as Everton and ABTA but, because nothing had been put in writing, there was little we could do.

Despite the excessive travelling, it was still a great trip although I took some stick for it and still do. Lads now call me 'Palma Padden' or 'Majorca Terry' and whenever I book any trips they ask 'Where are we going this time, Terry? You know, just so we know whether to bring our cosies and sun-tan lotions.'

Terry and co weren't the only ones making long journeys across Europe that month to follow the Blues.

Everton v Sunderland, 24 November 2007
The Dala Horse by Olof Schön

In 1970, English football began to be broadcast live on TV in my home country, Sweden. As a young boy you had to pick a favourite team and for me it was Everton. I did so for several reasons, notably the fact that we were champions that year and also because of Alan Ball and his performances for England.

Five years later, when the senior football team I played for travelled to England, I went to my first Everton game – a heavy 5-0 defeat to QPR at Loftus Road. I was the only boy from my team supporting Everton that day and the only supporter where I lived. Growing up as an Evertonian was a lonely experience. I think at one time I was the only Blue in the whole of Sweden – or so it felt like.

It wasn't until 2006 that I made my first visit to Goodison Park to introduce my ten-year-old son Martin to the Blues. By this time, several hundred Swedes were following the Toffees because of the team's success in the 1980s and the FA Cup win in '95, a game in which Sweden's Anders Limpar starred.

The following season I travelled for the Sunderland game with members of the Swedish Toffees, Everton's official supporters' club in Sweden. I had helped establish them with Per Malm to help Swedish Evertonians get to know each other and travel over for matches, as fans are scattered all over the country.

On Friday, 23 November, 15 of us travelled over to Merseyside for the home tie against Sunderland. After meeting at Manchester Airport, we made our way to Liverpool for a bespoke, half-day tour of Everton's history. We first visited Prince Rupert's Tower before moving on to Bellefield and the new training facility at Finch Farm. In between, we stopped off for a game of football in Kirkby on the site of the proposed new stadium before paying our respects to young Evertonian Rhys Jones in Croxteth.

Once the tour was over, we headed back to our hotel and into the city centre for a night out. At the end of the evening about five or six of us ended up in a Chinese restaurant. When I was returning to my seat after going to the toilet, I was stopped by a lady. She had spotted my Everton T-shirt which had 'Goodison Road' on and asked where I was from. During our conversation she showed me a picture of Dixie Dean's statue and asked if I had heard of the great man. Of course, I told her and was shocked when she said she was Dixie's youngest daughter, Barbara. When I heard this, I rushed over to the rest of our group, who returned with me to her table.

Her poor husband looked on as if to say 'Oh no, here we go again' as we chatted about Everton and, just like her father, you could tell she was a true Blue.

On match day, we went to Wetherspoon's 'The Thomas Frost', the Swedish Evertonians' favourite watering hole, for some pre-match food and ale.

Four of the Swedish Toffees committee then walked over to Goodison to present Tim Cahill with that year's Swedish Toffees award. The award was for the Everton player the Swedish Toffees felt had the biggest heart and Cahill had won this ahead of Stubbs, Carsley and Hibbert.

A representative from the club took us inside Goodison and in the main reception area we met Everton legend Duncan McKenzie. We were surprised that Duncan knew so much about Sweden, telling us how much he loved Swedish chocolate!

Thomas Gravesen then went past us and, when the Dane heard us speaking, asked 'Are you from Sweden?' in Swedish, before excusing himself to go in to prepare for the game.

Eventually we were led to a small room where we waited for our winner, Tim Cahill. When he entered the room he shook our hands before receiving his prize, a blue Dala Horse from our Chairman Erik Pråmell. The Dala Horse is a traditional Swedish souvenir and a national symbol. Erik explained what the award was for, and the Aussie, who seemed a bit surprised at first, was genuinely pleased. An official from the club took our photograph, which was later printed in the Oldham match programme, before Tim left to prepare for the game.

On our way out, we bumped into another legend, Graeme Sharp, who was also happy to chat and pose for photos, before we left to go back to Wetherspoon's.

When we took our seats in the Main Stand before kick-off, we bumped into Dixie Dean's daughter again. Barbara and the Dala Horse must have brought us luck that day as the game itself couldn't have been much better. We eventually put seven past the Black Cats, including a wonder goal from Leon Osman and a brace from the Dala Horse winner himself. The atmosphere was amazing with more than 35,000 Blues singing from start to end and afterwards we celebrated long into the night.

Overall, it turned out to be a memorable weekend watching the Blues which, like the great Dixie's record, will take some beating.

The highs of Nuremberg, a recordbreaking defeat of AZ Alkmaar (they were previously undefeated in Europe at home) and a 6-1 home drubbing of SK Brann were followed by a souldestroying exit in the last 16 at the hands of Fiorentina. The Blues lost on penalties despite clawing back a 2-0 firstleg deficit on a magical but ultimately disappointing night at Goodison.

Going into the 2008–09 season Everton fans were again hopeful of a sustained challenge in the League and to break into the top four, with Moyes having brought in some shrewd signings as well as breaking the transfer record for the fourth time with the purchase of Marouane Fellaini from Standard Liège, Everton's opponents in the UEFA Cup.

Standard Liège v Everton, 2 October 2008
Our Day Out by Colin Clarkson

Where do I start with Liège? I have never laughed as much in years as I did on that ferry.

We met up for breakfast and a few pints in Wetherspoon's in the morning and were picked up outside the Empire Theatre. Everyone ran the 50 yards to the coach, such was the excitement. This was like Our Day Out. I was just looking for the Everton Parrot.

The 'leader' of our group appeared to be a woman smashed off her face, which made for a grand start. Once we arrived at Hull, the group leaders were summoned into the terminal to try and thrash out a plan to get 240 of us on to the ferry.

After protracted negotiations, they came out of the terminal looking like a group of shop stewards leaving Laird's after a day of unsuccessful pay negotiations. We basically weren't getting on, as Hull had apparently 'never seen so many football fans'. Rubbish!

The leader of the ferry security was trying to placate some now irate Blues who were having a go at him, including smashed-out-of-her-head woman, who was a cross between Amy Winehouse on her best form and Ollie Reed. The next round of negotiations then commenced, with the ferry people now demanding we hand in our passports plus a £50 bond each. We disagreed, and it was settled that they should keep our passports.

The next problem was that they'd booked on only two coaches, not three. So they were frantically trying to get us all in cabins.

The captain was adamant we were sailing at 7 p.m. By about 6:15 p.m. those of us left were getting a bit twitchy. It became a case of telling them to 'just get us on the ferry and we'll kip on the deck if need be'. They then lobbed all those left into random cabins and it was sorted. We got the last Blues onboard, quite literally, about two minutes before the gangway was removed.

I'd just emptied my quite substantial holdall of all its contents before heading off to the bar – a toothbrush, tube of toothpaste and a can of deodorant – when my 'cabin buddy' then turned up. He was a young lad who weighed about seven stone wet through.

I introduced myself and jokingly mentioned that he looked similar to a lad I shared a cell with in Walton. Oh, he could call me Alice as well if he wanted. He turned the colour of boiled shite.

Once settled, we went up to the bar where there were 240 of us from the coaches, plus a load who'd made their own way there by car. I'd round it off to about 300 Evertonians. The beer was flowing, old acquaintances were remade, and then the singing started. It was a great atmosphere.

Then it happened: two or three hundred Blues, some of whom were older fellas from the '80s, switched off, shut up and settled down to a game of bingo.

It was the most surreal thing I've ever seen. Lads, who 20 or so years ago would've put you into next week, were all enjoying a good game of bingo. I was crying tears, absolute tears. The Blues were even 'singing' the numbers out to the bingo caller:

Two and 2 – 22 . . . 'Feed the Yak and he will score!'

Everyone behaved, no gobshites, nothing. It was just 300 Blues having a ball. The 'normal' people on the boat had no trouble at all and I saw loads getting on really well with the Blues. A lot of them even joined in.

The next morning we got up for some fresh air to find random Blues asleep on any bit of furniture available on the ferry. Madness. We were told by the captain to meet in the Moonlight Bar, where all our passports would be returned.

Once they had been given back, the captain came down to thank us for a great night, applaud us on how well behaved we were and say how much they enjoyed our company on the ship. He wished us well for the game and said, 'There are only two teams in Liverpool . . . Everton, and Everton reserves.'

Nice one, captain. It was ace when he said that. I know it was probably just relief that his ferry was still afloat, but it was a nice gesture nonetheless, and one he didn't have to make. It even made me feel quite proud.

We got to Liège and took a bus into town. It was miles away. There was a young woman on it carrying a Dead Kennedys DVD. I was contemplating trying to strike up a conversation and reference The Kennedys with her, but the big three-inch swastika tattooed on her forehead put me off.

Although I got into the ground, loads of Blues were locked out and it was half-time before everyone was in. It was an insipid and disappointing performance but I'll give Liège fans their due, they are one partisan bunch. I've not heard noise generated by a crowd of only twenty-odd thousand football fans like that in a long time. They were very, very impressive.

We got to Calais a little downhearted and boarded the ferry to Dover. We had a lovely greasy breakfast and then took the coach home to the 'Pool. We arrived back at midday on Friday and went straight back into Wetherspoon's, where it all started, for a pint and some scran. I then set off back home to a kiddies' birthday party for my son. I sat there looking like I'd just been dug up in St Chad's and placed on a chair.

To all the people on that ferry, I want to thank you for giving me one of the best nights of my life. I have never laughed that much for so long at anything to do with football. Good on you all. I've been all over with Everton, but that ferry ride I will take laughing to my grave with me.

A few weeks later, the entertainments manager off the ship emailed the organiser of our jaunt. The manager informed him that the P&O bar takings record for the Hull to Zeebrugge crossing had been smashed that night by a further £12,500. He also added that, like the great Dixie Dean's record, it would never be broken.

Standard Liège v Everton, 2 October 2008
Blues and Twos by Tom Sellick (no, not Magnum PI)

It was 10 a.m. on a Friday morning and I found myself running through Brussels Airport towards Gate 81 for my flight back to Manchester. My clothes were covered in blood and I was struggling to make any sort of progress with the stitches to my stomach I had received hours earlier in a Liege hospital. The last thing my dad had said to me before I left was, 'Well, it'll be an experience.' Little did I know just what an experience it would be.

We congregated outside Walton Hospital on the Wednesday evening full of optimism surrounding our European tour. Now, it's easy to see the irony of beginning the adventure in such a place; within 24 hours I'd be lying stricken on a hospital bed in agony.

The coach journey to Dover passed pretty quickly. The lads and

I had decided to make it to Belgium when we were heading home from Blackburn the week before. Neither that nor a numb derby performance could deter us. I'd had to pull out of the Nuremberg trip so I was making up for that and it was my first European away game.

The ferry over to France was not for the faint-hearted. We were rocking from side to side before we even set sail but Stella and Beck's helped to steady some stomachs at four in the morning. The lads were in good spirits though; sprawled out over the uncomfortable sofas and chairs on offer from P&O and eager to set up in Belgium.

France was a blur. The cheeky pints and the lack of sleep had got the better of most of us. Besides, saving energy was vital for what was to be a Thursday unlike the rest.

We arrived in Liège about 11 o'clock. We were offloaded at the craziest train station I've seen, then made our way through the puddle-riddled side streets towards anything that seemed to be the 'centre'. A few rogue directions later, we followed Scousers who seemed to be clued up and after passing caravans and funfair rides we arrived by the cathedral and bars.

First stop for me and my mates was to 'QUICK'. This fake Maccies was a weird one (paying to use the toilets, overpriced chips and a strange old woman showing us individually to the urinals). As soon as we left, we heard the first reverberations of Everton songs beckoning us to a Danish Bar on the corner. First pints of the day in and sorted in a prime location: happy days.

We walked round to the Irish bar on the other side of the town, but the distinct lack of bar staff led us to leave after a fruitless twenty minutes of waiting. I still can't remember the name of the bar we settled for; something in French I think. They had a beer called Maes though; avoid the peach-flavoured pint at all costs!

We were first to get the flag hung up, and it seemed to draw in other Blues. By 4.30 the place was booming. Every song in the book was coming out and it was around that time we decided to move into the centre. We found ourselves outside the Danish Bar once more, the streets were Royal Blue and some guy even started off with the flares. It was then that my European tour took a turn for the worse.

To gain a better view of the crowds I stood on the foundation of a local monument. As I jumped along with the singing, I lost my footing and caught my hip on the sharp corner of the stone base. I felt a sudden pain around my hip but as I was with the lads I decided to power through and not show much emotion. It was only when my mate pointed out the blood pouring down my leg that I started to worry and feel some pain. On lifting my jacket, I heard a few people around me say, 'He's been stabbed.'

Obviously I knew I hadn't but this idea seemed to gather pace. The next thing I knew I was lying on the pavement with the sirens of the ambulance on its way. I just wanted a bandage or something so I could get to the match but the chances of that happening soon vanished.

I arrived in the hospital to be grilled by two policemen. They were asking for the description of the face of the guy who stabbed me and what he was wearing. I was telling them what had happened but the doctors were insisting it was a stab wound.

Again I said it wasn't; again they looked at me curiously, spoke to each other in French and shook their heads. All the while, my best mate from school had been taken in for questioning by a couple more policemen. He was taken down to the station and quizzed before showing them his phone with photos of me on. 'Look, we're friends' seemed to do the trick and he was driven, siren-assisted, to the ground.

Meanwhile, my brother, a teacher, had received the news via mobile phone that I had 'been stabbed'. He later described it as the worst moment of his life; the fact that he was on a coach full of kids in the Lake District did little to comfort him. Thankfully, this 'Chinese whisper' was corrected before he aborted the trip.

So at the time of kick-off I was receiving several stitches. My ticket, with blood all over it, was still in my wallet. I demanded a TV in the room I was in. The cherry on the icing on the cake was to see the score. 0-1. Despite banging the bed in painful delight when Jagielka got one back, it was to be the camp male nurses who had the last laugh. 'You lose, my friend, you lose.'

After being released from hospital in the early hours, I flew back home via Brussels early on Friday morning. So the ongoing trauma of being an Evertonian continues and, after fifteen years, I've now got the physical scars to accompany the emotional ones. I'm sure some day somewhere I'll be able to say it was all worth it. Perhaps even on a balmy afternoon in May?

Once again, history had repeated itself as Everton were prematurely eliminated from Europe. Everton's fortunes turned around soon after. David Moyes signed his new contract and due to injuries, Mikel Arteta was moved into central midfield. This was to prove the catalyst for a fantastic run of results which again saw Everton threatening the top four. However, it was in the Cup where the biggest chance of silverware lay. In the run up to the Cup quarter final, the Blues had a tricky test away at Newcastle. Evertonians just hoped that everyone could come through unscathed, both fans and players alike.

Newcastle v Everton, February 22, 2009
This is the life by Jonathan Mumford

My alarm sounded at 7 a.m. For once I wasn't filled with dread of another long day in work. The alarm did, however, have a slightly musical quality, similar to when you hear Z Cars. I quickly remembered I was off to see the boys in blue away at Newcastle. We had been invited to travel to St James' by coach with the Southport Independent Blues and met up with Tony Prince in Birkdale, their usual pick up point. It was testament to Tony and the SIP that they turned out in such numbers so early on a Sunday for a game that was live on TV. We boarded the coach without fuss and the polite conversations ensued. 'Will it be like this all the way?' I wondered. My question was answered very quickly as it wasn't long before the songs about us going to Wembley boomed out. It's safe to say the excitement was building.

We arrived in Sunderland at a pre-arranged pub and met up with other Blues supporters' clubs. The lengths to which the supporters' clubs go in order to arrange a trip didn't go unnoticed. Collecting money, distributing tickets, chasing bad debtors and arranging coach hire are but a few of the tasks that must be addressed in preparation for a trip. We arrived at the pub a few hours before kick off to allow maximum consumption of alcohol, which, for many, was a lot. In the pub we met some characters; characters who exemplified dedication to the blue cause. We got talking to one fella who said he loved Everton so much that he had lost twelve jobs and two wives due to his 'obsession'. His wives said that he put Everton first. He even boasted that one ex gave him an ultimatum – go to watch Everton and sign the divorce papers she had left him. When signing the divorce papers, under his signature he wrote the words 'up the Toffees'! That sounded just about right. The pub was like a who's who of Everton fans. Barry Murray, from the Independent Blues, seemed to get a hero's welcome or a pat on the back whichever corner of the room he graced. When talking to him, he was quick to play down his status and was more concerned with drawing our attention to the older looking gentleman at the end of the bar. Barry went on to explain that Roy Gregory had only missed an unbelievable two games in fifty-two years. Fifty-two years! It would have been only one game had the coach not left him behind on an away trip a few years back! Such dedication and commitment makes you appreciate just how much Everton means to so many supporters.

Ignoring the fact that a group of younger blues were emptying the Pringle machine of all its contents, we were introduced to Mark Crosby. He had a tale to tell from a derby match in the mid-nineties. The weather that day was awful, a real storm, and it wasn't until just before kick off that the match was postponed. It was a big let down for everyone, especially for those who had warmed up for the game in the pubs around Goodison Park. Mark was one of those who set off home disappointed but with a belly full of beer. To get home, Mark had to negotiate the flower beds, trees and gravestones of Anfield cemetery in total darkness. This was easier said than done. Mark fell directly into an open grave. Not only that but, due to the severe weather conditions the grave was very muddy and he couldn't pull himself out. Wishing to conserve his energy he decided to get his head down for the night and try again in the early hours. When he awoke, and realised where he was, he began his struggle. Moaning and groaning as he climbed, and, sounding like a zombie by all accounts, he was greeted at the top by a very frightened couple who were walking through the cemetery. You can only guess what they were thinking when they saw a muddy body clambering from the grave.

In the pub, the beer was flowing at this stage and the singing really took off. I was surprised how few songs I recognised but, as Joe Royle said, the away fans are a special breed and make their own rules. With voices hoarse before the game had even started, it was back onto the coaches and up to St James'.

The game was a tightly fought draw but will unfortunately be remembered for two nasty incidents. One was the horrific tackle from Kevin Nolan which could easily have broken Victor Anichebe's leg. Nolan was sent off. The second was more significant. Everton's mercurial Spaniard Mikel Arteta twisted his knee and was stretchered off with barely five minutes on the clock and with it went Everton's creative spark. With an FA Cup quarter-final looming and a début appearance at the new Wembley a distinct possibility, this was a hammer blow to the Blues.

Despite the injury to our star player and a relatively dull game, the Evertonians were still in fine voice. There was not a seat to be had in the Everton section of the ground which is pretty much standard practice. Home teams cannot fail to be impressed with the loyalty and dedication shown by our fans week in week out in good times and bad. We have a special spirit and never seem to know when we're beaten neither as a team nor as supporters.

A 0-0 draw was the result but instead of being downhearted by the score line everyone's thoughts turned to the great FA Cup run. 'Tell me ma, me ma...' The singing recommenced and we set off for the long trip south. What struck me most about that trip with the Southport Independent Blues was the sheer loyalty to the club. Some people say that football is a religion. Now I know what they're talking about. I was blown away by the determination, good nature and collective mentality on display and feel proud to have been a part of it.

I'd loved to have played on Goodison Park again; it held so many fantastic memories for me. It's just a wonderful place to play. It was a wonderful place to play in front of people who appreciated people giving 100 per cent. That's what Goodison's all about, that's what the club's all about.

Alan Ball, interview, played on Everton TV, September 2008

Despite the setback of losing Arteta and Anichebe for the remainder of the season, Everton had something to cheer about when manager David Moyes and England defender Phil Jagielka were awarded February's Barclay's Manager and Player of the Month awards respectively. With injuries now commonplace, fans were hoping the players' commitment and team spirit would carry them into the semi-final of the FA Cup and to Wembley for the first time in fourteen years.

Middlesbrough were Everton's opponents for the quarter-final clash at Goodison Park on 8 March. In an earlier round Everton had defeated Liverpool thanks to a Dan Gosling strike just minutes from the end of extra time. Everton had earned a hard-fought 1-1 draw at Anfield and, in the replay, with Liverpool playing for penalties, the 18-year-old outfoxed three Liverpool defenders before curling the ball into the Park End net and, with it, etched his name in Goodison folklore.

After an in-form Aston Villa were dispatched 3-1, Everton were favourites to overcome 'Boro whose league form had seen them slip into the relegation zone. However, things don't always go according to form in the Cup and after a lacklustre first half by the Blues, they trailed the Teesiders 1-0 at half-time. At the interval, Moyes looked to Louis Saha for inspiration and the Frenchman duly obliged when he netted Everton's winner after Marouane Fellaini had equalised soon after the restart. The final whistle brought the Goodison faithful to their feet to celebrate Everton reaching their 24th FA Cup semi-final, to be played against Manchester United, the team they defeated in the semi-final of 1966 and the final in 1995.

Similar to the semi-final in 1995, when Everton faced Tottenham Hotspur, the Blues were the underdogs and keen to upset the media in their quest of the 'Dream Final'. Manchester United were chasing four trophies and sent out an under-strength but still very capable side. Opportunities were few and far between and, despite the Everton fans' rousing support, the game ended goalless after 90 minutes.

Extra time followed and was largely uneventful until a Leighton Baines cross found James Vaughan in the box, but the youngster scuffed his chance to seal a final place for the Blues. The semi-final was to be decided by the dreaded penalty shoot-out.

Tim Cahill courageously stepped up first, but blazed his shot over the bar. Evertonians felt the all-too-familiar pang of disappointment and prepared for the worst, especially as Everton's goalkeeper, Tim Howard, had not saved a penalty in his time at the club. However, the American certainly made up for that fact when he saved the following two Manchester United penalties. Eventually, it came down to one kick. Phil Jagielka, who had missed a penalty in the UEFA Cup shoot-out defeat to Fiorentina the previous season, was the man to take the kick. Evertonians held their breath. He sprinted up to the ball and buried it into the back of the Wembley net. Cue pandemonium. Everton had defeated the favourites and were in the FA Cup final for the 13th time.

Among the 35,000 delighted Everton fans that day were five Blues already on a high from the previous night's shenanigans.

FA Cup Semi-Final, Everton v Manchester Utd, Wembley, 19 April 2009
The Wedding Crashers by Mike Ford

It was our first trip to Wembley since '95. The FA, in their infinite wisdom, scheduled our game for the Sunday, so the five of us travelled down by car early Saturday morning to Cricklewood. We arrived at about 1 p.m. and checked into our hotel rooms. After unpacking, we all piled into one of the rooms and demolished a couple of crates of Beck's while watching the racing and latest football scores.

As it was quite early, we decided to have a look around Cricklewood, quaff more ale and watch the other semi-final. On leaving the hotel lift at reception we saw a bride and groom waiting outside. After offering our congratulations we got chatting to the happy couple. We discovered their names were Tom and Rose, wished them all the best and left to go and peruse the wonderful sights of Cricklewood.

After watching the semi, we returned to our rooms to shower and put on our gladrags – well, some of us did – Dave was, and is, the exception to the rule! So five hungry Blues then set off to find some grub and we happened on a Persian restaurant. After taking our seats, the waiter asked us if we would like a drink but to our horror no ale was served. After getting up off the floor and several 'Yer whats?' later one of our crowd recommended a drink called 'Doog'. What a disgusting drink – it tasted like piss!

After a couple more bars, we headed back to the hotel, pissed and tired but in good spirits as we looked forward to seeing our beloved Blues the next day. We decided on a nightcap in the lounge and then some much-needed kip when I noticed the disco lights shining out from above followed by the 'thump, thump' of some disco beat. We all looked at one another and declared, 'The wedding!' Without hesitation we agreed to give it a go and Jock and I went to test the water while the other three stayed to see how we got on.

As we went in, Tom, the groom, spotted us and came over looking like he was going to ask us to leave. We reminded him who we were and to our amazement said we had come to toast him and his new bride! He asked us to stay for one drink and left us to it. We ordered two bottles of Beck's and we were happy, with renewed thirst. It was then our night improved even further. The waiter told me it was a free bar! You can imagine the disappointment on my face! I then texted Keith with the words 'We're in and it's free ale.'

The other three arrived at the 'do' quicker than Usain Bolt. Collectively, we agreed to keep a low profile. Unfortunately, five pissed-up lads with the offer of free ale don't do low profile. We were soon up dancing, eating the buffet (which wasn't up to much to be honest) and getting pictures taken with the bride and groom.

One of the best moments was when Jock asked the DJ for Frankie Goes to Hollywood (he's of that age) and the DJ, being only about 25, didn't know whether it was the name of a group or a song!

At one point, my presence was challenged by a woman who asked whose side we were on, the bride's or groom's, to which I replied 'Both!' Sussing me out, she asked if we were down in London for the football and had just gate-crashed. I couldn't lie so admitted my guilt and expected a scream or bellow for security. Luckily, she simply said 'I thought so, only you cheeky Scouse bastards could do it and get away with it!'

We stayed until about 1.30 a.m., which coincidentally was when the free bar ended! Tom and Rose obviously saw their dream honeymoon to the Caymans turning into a wet weekend in Clapham if they carried on allowing us more free booze. We made our excuses and left, but obviously not before taking a few slices of wedding cake for later.

The next morning, at breakfast, and nursing bad hangovers, we regaled ourselves with the previous night's stories. After a relaxing swim and sauna we donned our blue and white regalia and headed to the nearest Wetherspoon's for more ale. It definitely doesn't taste the same when you have to pay for it! We headed to the tube at Willesden for the four-stop ride to Wembley and it was great to see the sight that greeted us – a sea of blue and white. The game was a blur – not because of the beer but from the sheer occasion of it all.

When penalties arrived, I couldn't bear to watch and spent the next ten minutes or so with my back to the play. I was just checking the reactions of those around me in blue and white. When Jagielka slotted the winner, along with thirty-odd thousand, I went mental. I don't mind admitting there was a tear or two in my eyes as there was with the other lads.

That night I think we were so exhausted both physically and mentally that we just let the whole experience wash over us. But there was still enough energy for more beer, of course. We retired back to the hotel, shattered but ecstatic before leaving for home on the Monday. It was a great weekend and on the way home we hoped for more of the same for the final come the 30th of May.

May 2009 saw Evertonians from across the land continue to demonstrate unconditional love for the club as they followed the Blues in their thousands to the new Wembley Stadium to roar on their team. Despite being allocated only 23,000 seats, well over 35,000 were believed to have got their hands on tickets.

David Moyes led out Everton on a sweltering day and the Blues wished for a good, solid start to the game. Twenty-five seconds into it Everton were 1-0 up. Louis Saha scored a fantastic left-footer and with it created history with the fastest ever Cup final goal.

What a start! The heat seemed to take its toll on the Blues rather more as Chelsea enjoyed the majority of possession and Everton chased shadows. Midway through the first half, Didier Drogba headed in a deserved equaliser and Everton looked jaded and out of ideas. Half-time came and went and after the restart, Everton began to keep the ball much better and created some opportunities. However, twenty minutes from full time, Frank Lampard lashed a left-foot strike into the top corner to leave Everton a mountain to climb. With time against them, the Blues didn't quite manage to break down an excellent Chelsea side and the game ended in a devastating defeat.

That day the boys in blue didn't quite manage to lift the famous trophy but it certainly gave the fans the taste for success. In spite of the narrow 2-1 defeat to Chelsea, one thing was for certain: come good times or bad, Evertonians will continue to follow their team. A club founded in 1878 which boasts more years in top-flight English football than any other. Such unrivalled loyalty demonstrates just what it means to be an Evertonian.

References

Graham, M. (1986) Everton, Hamlyn, Middlesex.

Keith, J. (2005) Colin Harvey's Everton Secrets, Trinity Mirror Sport Media, Liverpool.

Powter, D. (2002) 25 Seasons at Goodison: The Complete Record, Soccer Books, Cleethorpes.

www.bluekipper.com

www.evertonfc.com

www.evertonresults.com

www.toffeetalk.com

Acknowledgements

There are numerous people we would like to thank for helping us compile stories for this book.

In addition to all those who made contributions, we would also like to thank Vicky Ashworth, John Sellick, Steve Jones from Blue Kipper, Donnie 'Chubby' Stirrup, Gerry Foran, Ian Simpson (RCS), Andrew Calderbank, Ray Parr, John Keith, Mark O'Brien, Tony Prince and Graham Douglas.

More football books from SportsBooks

The Boys from the Black Country
Mark Gold

The author looks at the history of his club, Wolverhampton Wanderers, and his town with an affectionate and humorous eye. From Victorian times to the razzmatazz of the Premier League, *The Boys from the Black Country* tells the story of the club from the viewpoint of a fan and historian. This is football history with a difference. Alongside an original account of all the club's highs and lows Mark Gold brings a comic touch to parts of Wolves' glorious (and not so glorious) past. Where else could you find Geoffrey Boycott and Henry Blofeld commentating on the team's first FA Cup appearance in 1893, or discover what sort of terrace chant Wolves supporter Sir Edward Elgar might compose were he alive today?

ISBN 9781899 96 3
£7.99
Paperback

Stan Anderson – captain of the north

Stan Anderson is the only man to have captained the north east's three big clubs – Sunderland, Newcastle and Middlesbrough. Indeed only three players have played for all three. Stan was also a member of the England squad for the 1962 World Cup in Chile and he remembers the great players he played alongside such as Duncan Edwards and Bobby Charlton. His stories of financial double dealing by Sunderland shows just how players were treated as serfs in the 1950s and '60s. Written with Mark Metcalf.

ISBN 9781899807 98 7
£17.99
Hardback

Scouting for Moyes
Les Padfield

All football clubs have them – scouts. Men (for they are almost always men) who watch teams to check how they play, who watch players to see how good they are. Even in these high tech days of video analysis and Prozone (a system which tells how far each player has run in a game, how many passes and how successful they were etc.) football clubs could not operate without the human element of scouting.

Les Padfield, though, is not your typical scout. Not many are published poets! A Londoner, he was a schoolboy footballer of great promise – as he writes, Harry Redknapp, the Spurs manager, used to provide the crosses for him to score when they were schoolboys. He chose though to become a teacher of Physical Education, English and other subjects. He became a scout when, having been persuaded to attend a match at Millwall he meets an old friend, John Sainty, the chief scout at Preston North End. Sainty tells Les that the club's manager, David Moyes, is looking for a London-based scout. And even though Les moved on to Bolton Wanderers in the Premier League, the title 'Scouting for Moyes' was too good to resist.

Les tells of the frustrations of the job, the perks – a trip to Nigeria to watch a teenage prodigy who revealed he preferred to study medicine – and the precarious nature of football life. Gary Megson, Bolton's manager who had also employed Les when he was in charge at West Bromwich Albion and Nottingham Forest, is sacked at the end of 2009. Les also offers the insight of a professional into the world,of football. Surprisingly his views are very often those of an outright fan.

ISBN 9781899 95 6
£8.99
Paperback

The Teams of Sunderland AFC
Paul Days and Brian Leng
The authors, both long-time Sunderland supporters who have contributed to many books over the years, have collected together as many of Sunderland AFC team photographs as they could find. The first is from 1884–85 and the latest from 2010. This is a true labour of love and a great historical record.

ISBN 9781899807 97 0
£25.00
Hardback

The FA Cup 50 Years On
Mark Metcalf
When Wolverhampton Wanderers beat Blackburn Rovers 3-0 in the 1960 FA Cup final, the competition was king. Players preferred an FA Cup winners medal to topping the League. Mark Metcalf spoke to

players and fans involved in the final to paint a picture of the FA Cup that year and the final in particular.

ISBN 9781899807 91 8
£7.99
Paperback

Finn McCool's Football Club
Stephen Rea

After jetting around the world, Stephen Rea left his hometown of Belfast with his American wife to settle in New Orleans in 2004. Not surprisingly, life in the Deep South proved to be startlingly different from that in Northern Ireland, and Rea struggled to find an outlet for his love of football. But before long the Ulsterman stumbled upon Finn McCool's pub and the wonderfully eccentric, international crowd that gathers there to watch European football games. Soon Rea and this idiosyncratic mix of locals and ex-pat regulars formed a pub soccer team, joined a league, and began dreaming of victory.

On August 27, 2005 members of the team sat in the pub discussing their upcoming match. The next day, Hurricane Katrina enveloped the Gulf Coast, scattering Rea and his teammates around the world in seek of shelter and stability.

This luminous, gripping work follows the author and Finn regulars as they rebuild their lives and their team. With a masterful combination of dry humour and astute profundity, Rea reflects on his adopted city, providing powerful insights into the lives of the foreign-born and minority groups that stayed behind during Katrina because they had little to lose. 'Finn McCool's Football Club' stands out as a haunting and powerful memoir filled with laughter, loss, astonishment, and, of course, football.

ISBN 9781899807 86 4
Price £8.99
Paperback

William Garbutt – the Father of Italian Football
Paul Edgerton

Born in Stockport, William Garbutt was a successful winger with Blackburn Rovers in the First Division, having first played for Woolwich Arsenal, when injury finished his career at the age of 29. He was good enough to have played for the Football League against the Scottish League in 1910. The usual route for ex-professionals was to become a publican but in 1912 Garbutt moved to Italy and took charge of Genoa Cricket and Football Club. In doing so he became the first professional football manager in Italian football. His professionalism and revolutionary ideas had a great impact on the club and under his guidance Genoa won the Italian League Championship three times – in 1915, 1923 and 1924. Garbutt is still considered an icon in Genoese football circles and is the reason why, to this day, Italian players call their manager 'Mister'.

In 1927 he joined the newly formed AS Roma and guided them to a cup win in his first season. He then moved to Napoli for six seasons, taking them to third position in the league - the highest spot they had ever enjoyed and which they only bettered many years later. Garbutt repeated his remarkable success on moving to Spain in 1935, where he guided Athletic Bilbao to the championship of the Spanish League before returning to his first love, Genoa, shortly afterwards. As a British citizen he was an exile under Mussolini's fascists and was interned during World War II, with the cruel irony that his wife, Anna, was killed by Allied bombing. He returned to England in the late 1940s and died in 1964 in Warwick. Author Paul Edgerton traced his adopted daughter Maria, who sadly passed away in August 2009, for a unique insight into an extraordinary man.

ISBN 9781899807 82 6
Price £7.99
Paperback

Passport to Football
Stuart Fuller

Well-known blogger Stuart Fuller is a member of a growing band of thousands of football fans who, growing tired of watching an over-hyped and over-priced Premier League and taking advantage of cut-price travel, enjoys watching his favourite game in different countries.

This is not simply a reference guide, more a travelogue – a book that traces the journeys Fuller takes for football, whether with England, where he has been a far from successful manager of the England Fans senior team, or on a whim. He has watched matches in places as diverse as Moscow, Macedonia, Tallinn, Palermo, Zagreb, Florida, Amsterdam, Tel Aviv, Andorra, Zurich, Copenhagen, Vienna, Stockholm, Monaco, Salzburg, Istanbul, Bremen, Paris, Krakow, Minsk, Sofia, Naples, Skopje and Barcelona.

Anyone wanting to follow in his footsteps will be able to use the book as a guide but will also enjoy Fuller's account of dealing with Easyjet and Ryanair, sorting out the purchase of tickets in foreign lands and 'collecting' football stadiums. You will meet Fuller's list of fellow travellers, including Football Jo, Dagenham Dan, Big Ben and Rob the Red. They steer clear of the trouble that frequently accompanies the England football team on its travels, enjoying sightseeing as well as beer and sausages.

9781899807 83 3
Price £12.99
Paperback

Chapped Legs and Punctured Balls

Paul Cooper lived for football like most other 1960s kids and this is his account, both hilarious and nostalgic, of the things that went with the game in those more innocent times – the clothes and shoes kids wore, the balls they played with, from the very rare leather case ball with its occasionally crippling lace to the stone that was used in the playground if nothing else was available.

9781899807 77 2
£5.99
Paperback

Modern Football is Rubbish

Nick Davidson & Shaun Hunt

The authors are going through a midlife crisis as far as football is concerned. Now they've reached early middle-age they are wondering what has happened to the beautiful game. Where have all the muddy pitches gone they wonder. They wallow in nostalgia for 3 p.m. Saturday kick-offs and cup upsets and they rant against inflated egos, spiralling salaries and satellite TV. And they wonder about men in tights and gloves. "Poignant and thought-provoking book... it strikes just the right tone throughout, somewhere between gentle nostalgia and constructive criticism; has many laugh-out-loud moments yet poses some serious questions..." Jon Crampin, FourFourTwo magazine.

9781899807 71 0
Price £7.99
Paperback

Modern Football is STILL Rubbish

Nick Davidson & Shaun Hunt

The authors, their midlife football crisis far from over, found they couldn't get all they had to say into just one volume. So they turned their judgement on more of the game's sacred cows. FourFourTwo magazine's Jon Crampin was just as impressed with the follow-up: "This book is just as thought-provoking as the original, but if anything, even more poignant in the light of football's impending financial meltdown."

9781899807 90 1
Price £7.99
Paperback

The World at their Feet: Northern Ireland in Sweden
Ronnie Hanna
The story of Northern Ireland's first trip to the World Cup finals when, despite being the smallest country, they reached the quarter-finals. Ronnie Hanna also wrote *Six Glorious Years: Following Northern Ireland 1980– 86.* "Now a local author, Ronnie Hanna, has produced a definitive record of that era... It is a must for Northern Ireland football fans. I enjoyed every minute perusing (it). An immense amount of research has been undertaken... making the end product a fascinating story," Malcolm Brodie, *Belfast Telegraph.*

9781899807 74 1
Price £7.99
Paperback

From Sheffield with Love
Brendan Murphy
October 2007 was the 150th anniversary of the founding of Sheffield FC and there was considerable celebration both in England and among the wider footballing and sporting community, with Inter Milan, AC Milan, Real Madrid and Barcelona involved. In recognition of their unique position as the world's oldest football club, Sheffield FC were awarded a FIFA Centenary Order of Merit in 2004. Only one other team in the world have been similarly honoured: Real Madrid.

Sheffield is the true birthplace of football, having a huge influence on the Football Association after the Sheffield Football Association was once a rival to the game's ruling body.

The book is packed with fascinating facts and trivia about the birth of football. It is both fun and educational. It should attract not only football fans but lovers of sport in general

9781899807 56 7
Price £8.99
Paperback

The Irish Uprising

Andy Dawson

Although Sunderland were relegated from the Premiership in 2006 with a record-low 15 points things were looking up when an Irish consortium headed by former centre forward Niall Quinn assumed control at the Stadium of Light. But Quinn could not find a manager and with Quinn as manager as well as chairman they lost their first five games including an FA Cup defeat by Bury from the lowest Division. But Quinn persuaded his former Irish teammate Roy Keane to take over. With Keane, renowned throughout a long, distinguished career, spotted with controversy, for his uncompromising attitude, sitting in the stands Sunderland beat West Bromwich Albion. Keane signed as manager and the ex-Manchester United hard-man has led the charge up the league to automatic promotion. Much has happened at the Stadium of Light since then but Keane's firsts season was still a remarkable effort.

9781899807 60 4
Price £10.99
Paperback

Growing up with Subbuteo: my Dad invented the world's greatest football game

Mark Adolph

Mark Adolph was the envy of his schoolmates – he never had any problem getting rare Subbuteo teams because his Dad invented the game and owned the factory that made it.

Mark tells the story of Subbuteo from the very early days when his father Peter had thousands of orders but no games with which to supply them. He recounts his father's adventures in football as a director of Tonbridge FC and supporter of Queens Park Rangers, as an avid collector of luxury cars and as "a bit of a rogue".

Peter began his adventure with an advertisement in *Boys Own* magazine in 1947 offering a new table top football game for 7/6d (37.5p in new money). At that time it was just an idea but soon began the frantic process of making the game and suggesting it should be played on a pitch made from an old Army blanket!

1899807 40 3
Price £7.99
Paperback